THE *Art*
OF *Creative*
Writing

Other books by Lajos Egri

YOUR KEY TO SUCCESSFUL WRITING
THE ART OF DRAMATIC WRITING

THE *Art*
OF *Creative*
Writing

by LAJOS EGRI

THE CITADEL PRESS
Secaucus, N. J.

For my beloved Father and Mother

Contents

THE *Art*
OF *Creative*
Writing

1

Universal Man:
The Art of Enduring Writing

In this book my aim is to give the writer an understanding of human behavior and to show how he can apply it in his work. Every type of creative writing depends upon the credibility of a character. This is why a writer must know when a character is one-, two- or three-dimensional.

Men are essentially the same. The difference is only in degrees. All this sounds simple enough, but the problem is how to capture this chameleon-like creature in repose long enough to draw his true image. What the writer wants to know is how a real human being—a three-dimensional character—acts in life. The answer is simplicity itself: like you or me.

"Yes," one may argue, "but I really don't know how I act. One day this way, another day the opposite. Does it make sense?" Of course it does. Every human being is as contradictory as you and I. We constantly vacillate. Sometimes you and I are very much alike, and sometimes we are worlds apart.

There was a great furor, which to this day has not abated, when Freud discovered the id and the superego—the subconscious mind of man. Yet, as literary scholars know, the writers of the past were the real discoverers of the workings of the mind.

No doubt they closely watched people around them acting in real life. They must have been appalled by their contrariness! The more they watched, the more disturbed they must have become.

They must have found contradiction in everything man did. To this very day we cannot find any living human being who we can claim is angelic through and through or rotten to the core.

This knowledge was surely one of the greatest discoveries in the age foreshadowing Freud, Jung, Adler and the rest.

Yes, man is complex. The truth is—man has the capacity to be heroic, superhuman, ready to sacrifice his life for an ideal and with the same ease, cut his best friend's throat.

In short: he's good and evil at the same time. It depends on what inner or outside contradiction activates him to expose himself.

This sounds too general to be of great help for a writer interested in character building. I must be more concrete, more personal. I will take one man, a character, vivisect him to see the nakedness, the complexity, the contradiction in his mind. Since I know myself better than anyone alive, I will give you the summation of my character.

(After you finish reading the following, please remember what Jesus said: "Let him without sin cast the first stone.")

I am greedy, selfish, and jealous and I try desperately to be loved by all. I am thinking day and night of how to make myself so important that it will force people to think only good about me. I am sorry, but it's true that I always want to be in the right.

I came to the conclusion that whatever I say, I say for only two reasons:

1. To create sympathy for myself.
2. To show how important I am.

This is what I found inside myself. At first, it was frightening. "I cannot be this!" I cried. I looked again and saw the same. It is true. I am all that and more.

All great character portraits were and will be written with the detachment of a dedicated scientist—determined to tell the truth and nothing but the truth whoever will be hurt in the process.

Only a corpse can exist without contradiction. The corpse is busy disintegrating, while a living man is preoccupied with the struggle to keep soul and body together. This is, in itself, a Herculean job to accomplish.

The universal man is really the average man. The difference between him and his superior brother, the genius, is only in degrees. We are, after all, brothers under the skin. If you truly know one—you know all.

2

What Is Originality?

Editors, publishers, and producers are eternally on the lookout for an "original" story or play. They talk glibly about this precious quality as if it might be found in any ash can or any corner.

Originality, however, like genius, must be rare. Still, competent people, especially leaders in the literary field, use the word promiscuously.

"I consider even an old, down-at-the-heels situation original if it has a new, fresh treatment," a well-known novelist has said.

Another notable said, "Put in more pep; a new twist will lift up your second and third acts. A few clever lines, aglow with originality, wouldn't be amiss either."

Such talk is sheer nonsense. What is a new twist to you may be an old twist to somebody else. The same goes for questionable clever lines or so-called fresh treatment.

"Fresh treatment" is merely rearrangement; the face-lifting may tighten a line here and there, but it creates nothing original.

I heard one dramatist say, "Originality is something we cannot profane with a definition. You simply feel it. It is something like an aroma. You can't touch it with your fingertips. Perhaps 'unique' is the word, I don't know. A spark out of the author's genius might light up a piece of writing so that it'll dazzle you with its brilliance."

It would have been helpful of him to tell young writers how to create such an "aroma" . . . that untouchable something.

If we want a definition of originality, our best method is to take a masterpiece, whether a play, novel or short story, and see where this or that giant of literature carries its originality.

War and Peace by Tolstoy; *The Diamond Necklace* by de Maupassant, *The Gift of the Magi* by O. Henry, are a few of the works which readers treat with special respect.

The plots in these stories are not extraordinary either. The themes are just as orthodox. The question is—what makes them so enduring? Why do they defy time?

If you reread them, you will be forcibly reminded of one thing—each one is outstanding for its *character portrayals.* The characters are people whom we know; perchance we recognize ourselves in them. The authors apparently knew their characters intimately and, with a few bold strokes or with detailed drawing, made them come to life.

Origin means the beginning of something—something that did not exist before. Here are a few examples: The concepts of monotheism, of relativity; the invention of the linotype; the wheel.

Leeuwenhoek was original with his microscope. Making a fire was an absolutely original contribution.

Twenty-five hundred years ago, Zeno presented an absolutely new dialectical approach to man and to the world. Descartes, Feuerbach, Hegel and Marx accepted Zeno's basic dialectical principle but they interpreted it differently. Did this make them original too? While the first three explained the world in terms of idealism, Marx turned their idealistic interpretation on its head, so to speak, and created the most controversial philosophy in the world, dialectical materialism.

If we are to keep originality on the high level to which it rightfully belongs, we must admit that Descartes, Feuerbach and Hegel were not original thinkers.

But let us pursue the definition of originality in writing. A new approach, one might say.

If we insist that original must mean that no one has ever used that theme or style before, not one play by Shakespeare, Molière or Ibsen is original. In that sense, the themes or styles of these authors are certainly not original, for they have been used from time immemorial.

No doubt Jesus, Darwin, and Marx were advocators of new, revolutionary thoughts. Copernicus, Galileo, Newton, and Einstein all brought something restlessly new to human knowledge. Faraday, Tesla and Edison were in the first rank of the originators of physics. Galen and Hippocrates were the pioneers in medicine. Nietzsche's *Zarathustra* foreshadowed Adolf Hitler, the destroyer of civilization.

In art, Matisse discarded the familiar precepts of painting and created a revolution with his flat patterns; Cézanne was the forerunner of Cubism, and Picasso the creator of many a new "ism." Seurat was the originator of pointillism. El Greco became known as the father of the elongated style.

The sum total of all this is that in the arts there are originators of *new slants, new approaches, new surprising twists,* but very few artists ever bring forth such original creations as Einstein's relativity.

Originality, like genius, is rare.

No matter what we think of Gertrude Stein or E. E. Cummings, and others of their kind, we must still consider them the creators of something so radically new, so different, that we have to give them the doubtful distinction of originality. But they are not necessarily great. Far from it.

We once heard about a mad genius who discovered a new, distinct type of airplane—an absolutely revolutionary airplane—one that couldn't fly. It was certainly original!

However, one must not detract from the achievements of man. Nature is full of many astounding and original ideas, which existed before a homo sapien ever put in an appearance on this globe. The manner in which man has solved some of these mysteries is little less than miraculous.

Still, *originality* must mean the *beginning* of something.

In the arts however, we cannot discover startling originality—only trends, styles, twists, slants, tricks, exaggeration, minimization, emphasis on parts instead of a whole. Originality, then, is rare in the field of literature and, for that matter, in all fields of art.

If we consider originality almost non-existent, then what shall a writer strive for? Characterization. Living, vibrating human beings are still the secret and magic formula of great and enduring writing. Read, or better, study the immortals and you will be forced to conclude that their unusual penetration into human character is what has kept their work fresh and alive through centuries, and not because they may have used a new "slant" which seemed to many to be "original."

3

Emotion:
Source of Reader Identification

Great stories or plays do not necessarily deal with outlandish characters. What makes a story great is that we recognize the characters as real flesh-and-blood human beings.

In ancient Greece, someone told Socrates that the Oracle had just declared him the wisest man of Athens. Socrates could not believe this, but the friend insisted it was true. Socrates was always a very thorough man, and he wished to find out if the Oracle could have made a mistake. He asked poets, politicians, plain people in the street and, at last, philosophers whether each would consider himself the wisest man in Athens. Without exception each one said yes, he would. Socrates sadly concluded that the Oracle must have been right. "At least I know how little I know."

Yes, the knowledge of how little he knows makes even a great writer humble in the throes of creation.

A skeptic may ask the pertinent question, "Where is that hidden power in a character that, realized as you say it should be realized, will astound us with its novelty?"

I saw that identification is the touchstone and the answer. The same skeptic might ask again, "Where is the law that says a story should be exciting just for the simple reason that the author succeeded in creating a recognizable human being?''

Here is where the writer's intelligence is tested to the full. The first step is to make your reader or viewer identify your character as someone he knows. Step two—if the author can make the audience imagine that what is happening can happen to him, the situation will be permeated with aroused emotion and the viewer will experience a sensation so great that he will feel not as a spectator but as the participant of an exciting drama before him.

I've heard writers talk glibly about this mysterious phenomenon of identification, but they never could explain satisfactorily what it is and how it is achieved.

It *is* a pity, because to write successfully one must be able to create identification. Without this skill, the writer will work in a vacuum and never know why he failed. But it is not enough to memorize the tricks of a profession. He must understand and know character first of all.

Here is a short episode from Ibsen's *Hedda Gabler*. The first scene does a wonderful job of creating identification between the audience and the characters.

Miss Tesman, with her bonnet and parasol, comes to greet the returning honeymooners, her nephew George and Hedda, his bride. George is delighted to see her. He should be. After all, old Miss Tesman took care of him all his life and now, to please the newlyweds, has given him money from her small annuity for their new furniture. She is full of admiration and the best of intentions toward them.

Hedda enters from the left through the inner room. She is a woman of twenty-nine. Her face and figure show refinement and distinction. Her complexion is pale and opaque. Her steel-gray eyes express a cold, unruffled repose. Her hair is of an agreeable medium brown, but not particularly abundant. She is dressed in a tasteful, somewhat loose-fitting morning gown.

MISS TESMAN (*going to meet Hedda*): Good morning, my dear Hedda! Good morning and a hearty welcome.

HEDDA (*holds out her hand*): Good morning, dear Miss Tesman! So early a call! That is kind of you.

MISS TESMAN (*with some embarrassment*): Well—has the bride slept well in her new home?

HEDDA: Oh yes, thanks. Passably.

TESMAN (*laughing*): Passably! Come, that's good, Hedda! You were sleeping like a stone when I got up.

HEDDA: Fortunately. Of course, one has always to accustom oneself to new surroundings, Miss Tesman—little by little. (*Looking toward the left*): Oh—there the servant has gone and opened the verandah door, and let in a whole flood of sunshine.

MISS TESMAN (*going toward the door*): Well, then, we will shut it.

HEDDA: No, no, not that! Tesman, please draw the curtains. That will give a softer light.

TESMAN (*at the door*): All right—all right. There now, Hedda, now you have both shade and fresh air.

HEDDA: Yes, fresh air we certainly must have, with all these stacks of flowers—But—won't you sit down, Miss Tesman?

MISS TESMAN: No, thank you. Now that I have seen that everything is all right here—thank heaven!—I must be getting home again. My sister is lying longing for me, poor thing.

TESMAN: Give her my very best love, Auntie, and say I shall look in and see her later in the day.

MISS TESMAN: Yes, yes, I'll be sure to tell her. But by-the-by, George—(*feeling in her dress pocket*) I have something for you here.

TESMAN: What is it, Auntie? Eh?

MISS TESMAN (*produces a flat parcel wrapped in newspaper and hands it to him*) : Look here, my dear boy.

TESMAN (*opening the parcel*): Well, I declare! Have you really saved them for me, Aunt Julia! Isn't this touching—eh?

HEDDA (*beside the whatnot on the right*): Well, what is it?

TESMAN: My old morning shoes! My slippers.

HEDDA: Indeed. I remember you often spoke of them when we were abroad.

TESMAN: Yes, I missed them terribly. (*Goes up to her*) Now you shall see them, Hedda!

HEDDA (*going towards the stove*): Thanks, I really don't care about it.

TESMAN (*following her*): Only think—ill as she was, Aunt Rina embroidered these for me. Oh, you can't think how many associations cling to them.

HEDDA (*at the table*): Scarcely for me.

MISS TESMAN: Of course not for Hedda, George.

TESMAN: Well, but now she belongs to the family, I thought—

HEDDA (*interrupting*) : We shall never get on with this servant, Tesman.

MISS TESMAN: Not get on with Berta?

TESMAN: Why, dear, what put that in your head? Eh?

HEDDA (*pointing*): Look there! She has left her old bonnet lying about on a chair.

TESMAN (*in consternation, drops the slippers to the floor*): Why, Hedda—

HEDDA: Just fancy, if anyone should come in and see it!

TESMAN: But Hedda—that's Aunt Julia's bonnet.

HEDDA: It is!

MISS TESMAN (*taking up the bonnet*): Yes indeed it's mine. And, what's more, it's not old, Madame Hedda.

HEDDA: I really did not look at it closely, Miss Tesman.

MISS TESMAN (*trying on the bonnet*): Let me tell you it's the first time I have worn it—the very first time.

TESMAN: And a very nice bonnet it is too—quite a beauty.

MISS TESMAN: Oh, it's no such great thing, George. (*Looks around her*): My parasol—? Ah, there. (*takes it*) For this is mine too— (*mutters*) not Berta's.

TESMAN: A new bonnet and a new parasol! Only think, Hedda!

HEDDA: Very handsome indeed.

TESMAN: Yes, isn't it? Eh? But Auntie, take a good look at Hedda before you go! See how handsome she is!

MISS TESMAN: Oh, my dear boy, there's nothing new in that. Hedda was always lovely. (*She nods and goes toward the right*)

TESMAN (*following*): Yes, but have you noticed what splendid condition she is in? How she has filled out on the journey?

HEDDA (*crossing the room*): Oh, do be quiet—!

MISS TESMAN (*who has stopped and turned*): Filled out?

TESMAN: Of course you don't notice it so much now that she has that dress on. But I, who can see—

HEDDA (*at the glass door, impatiently*): Oh, you can't see anything.

TESMAN: It must be the mountain air in the Tyrol—

HEDDA (*curtly, interrupting*): I am exactly as I was when I started.

TESMAN: So you insist, but I am quite certain you are not. Don't you agree with me, Auntie?

MISS TESMAN (*who has been gazing at her with folded hands*): Hedda is lovely—lovely—lovely. (*Goes up to her, takes her head between both hands, draws it downwards, and kisses her hair*) God bless and preserve Hedda Tesman—for George's sake.

HEDDA (*gently freeing herself*): Oh—! Let me go.

MISS TESMAN (*in quiet emotion*): I shall not let a day pass
without coming to see you.

TESMAN: No, you won't, will you Auntie? Eh?

MISS TESMAN: Goodbye—goodbye! (*she goes out by the hall
door.*)

How can a young man, in any country today, identify himself with Miss Tesman? He seems to have nothing whatever
in common with her. Did I make a mistake in quoting the
above as an example of identification? I don't think so. The
young man *does* share one thing with Miss Tesman. At some
time in his life he has been humiliated.

Miss Tesman has been humiliated by the proud, self-
centered Hedda. All of Hedda's frustration at marrying a
man like George Tesman has become venom poured out on
the head of an innocent old lady who has nothing but love in
her heart.

Her humiliation arouses spontaneous identification in us.
It starts in the subconscious. We pity Miss Tesman and despise Hedda. Why? For a very simple reason: Every grown
person has felt the sting of humiliation at least once during
his lifetime.

Humiliation in this case is the touchstone in what we call
identification. Humiliation is universal and timeless.

Identification can be established easily if the characters
create emotion which we recognize at once.

Identification is important not only in the theatre or in
any type of fiction but in our everyday lives. We meet a
stranger. After a quick look, the so-called first impression is
formed. It may be violent dislike, even though the stranger is
well-dressed, polite, even kind to us. Why?

We never forget unkindness, embarrassment, neglect or
cruelty, and if the unfortunate stranger reminds us subconsciously of someone who behaved badly to us in the past, our

hostility will be immediate—and almost irrevocable. A trace of resentment can linger for years in the subconscious and on the slightest provocation call forth a reaction to someone we never saw before.

And in writing, as in life, identification must be established through emotion. If the author shows us an unscrupulous individual, he should take it for granted that the reaction will be unfavorable toward the character. The logical question now is whether everybody's reaction will be the same. The answer is, without a doubt, yes.

You may disagree. Let me remind you that we are dealing here with universal emotions such as love, hate, jealousy, fear, greed. The audience's reaction will depend upon the writer. If the character is not fully realized the reaction will be nil.

One might object that a play or a story cannot start at the height of an emotion. Granted, but then you must have suspense, suggestion that the story or play will grow in intensity. Emotion without suspense is wasted energy, and we had better remember that there is no suspense without emotion.

In Lillian Hellman's *The Little Foxes,* Birdie, a young but weak and frightened woman, is talking to Cal, a Negro servant, as the dining-room doors are opened and quickly closed by Oscar Hubbard, Birdie's husband.

CAL: Yes'm. But Simon, he won't get it right. But I'll tell him.

BIRDIE: Left drawer, Cal, and tell him to bring the blue book —and—

OSCAR (*sharply*): Birdie.

BIRDIE (*turning nervously*): Oh, Oscar, I was just sending Simon for my music album.

OSCAR (*to Cal*): Never mind about the album. Miss Birdie has changed her mind.

BIRDIE: But really, Oscar. Really, I promised Mr. Marshall I— (*Cal looks at them, exits*)

OSCAR: Why do you leave the dinner table and go running about like a child?

BIRDIE (*trying to be gay*): But Oscar, Mr. Marshall said most specially he *wanted* to see my album. I told him about the time Mama met Wagner, and Mrs. Wagner gave her the signed program, and the big picture. Mr. Marshall wants to see that. Very, very much. We had such a nice talk—

OSCAR (*taking a step to her*): You have been chattering to him like a magpie. You haven't let him be for a second. I can't think he came South to be bored with you.

BIRDIE (*quickly hurt*): He wasn't bored. I don't believe he was bored. He's a very educated, cultured gentleman. (*Her voice rises*) I just don't believe it. You always talk like that when I'm having such a nice time.

OSCAR (*turning to her, sharply*): You have had too much wine. Get yourself in hand now.

BIRDIE (*drawing back, about to cry, shrilly*): What am I doing? I'm not doing anything. What am I doing?

OSCAR (*taking a step to her, tensely*): I said get yourself in hand. Stop acting like a fool.

BIRDIE (*turns to him quietly*): I don't believe he was bored. I just don't believe it. Some people like music and like to talk about it. That's all I was doing.

No doubt about it, we are moved to anger by Oscar Hubbard's brutality. A little while later he'll slap her face. We wouldn't be human if we didn't want to see Oscar beaten as he deserves. Again, emotion has catapulted us to anger, and we are eager to see justice done, which is suspense.

Tennessee Williams' *Glass Menagerie* is another good example of identification. The mother's anxiety for her crippled daughter is contagious.

Arthur Miller's *Death of a Salesman* portrays frustration leading to suicide. No human being can remain indifferent to Willy Loman's pathetic dreams. We readily identify ourselves with this man. We start to worry about dreams—our lives.

Curiosity is also an emotion. We feel curiosity about Sartre's *No Exit*. Characters live in "Hell" here, but this Hell is more devastating than the old "Inferno" of Dante. Unfulfilled emotion is worse than the iron tongue. Then comes monotony, boredom, the cruelest torture that any man ever conceived. "There's no need for red-hot pokers. Hell is—other people." We shall watch such a play with mounting horror.

Let me repeat once more that identification is emotion. You might start gently to arouse emotion in us, but your success or failure will depend on whether you can sustain the rising emotion which also corresponds with rising suspense.

And now a few words about the origin of emotion. Why has emotion such fatal power over our lives and, finally, why do other peoples' misfortunes arouse in us such thunderous reaction?

Fear for their lives drove our forefathers to live in the trees, and hunger and fear drove them down to the ground once more.

Although we think of fear as a concept, something we cannot touch, the moment it permeates our consciousness it becomes a dreadful reality, causing real pain. Fear is a universal emotion and one of the deadliest of all human experiences. But this singular emotion is responsible for man's survival.

It is paradoxical but true that hate or love, treachery or loyalty, spring from one and the same source—insecurity. Emotion then is a thousand-pronged weapon to safeguard our lives. It spells out for our survival the basic tenet of our experience, insecurity, and now it has become a truism that life would be impossible without that insecurity of which we are so mortally afraid. Insecurity gives impetus to inventors to safeguard our existence.

But insecurity, like the mighty atom, can disguise itself as any one of an endless variety of things. It is almost impossible to recognize the naked fear behind the disguise of, let's say, philanthropy.

It is almost brash to say that philanthropy—a beautiful gesture, a sign of understanding, love—is the outgrowth of fear. But if I follow up this reasoning, which I propose to do, I will show that all human emotion and conflict, whether personal, national, or international, spring from the same source—insecurity.

Logic doesn't always have a chance to win against emotion, because emotion has the power to melt even granite and make prejudice blush with shame. It is the most potent weapon man can wield against man, the prime power behind all human conduct. Reason may triumph in the end but emotion will carry a project to success.

But emotion is one more thing: it is an invisible chain, linking man to man all over the globe. Danger, any kind of danger that can imperil the life of a man even at a thousand miles' distance, is a potential enemy to us all. If a murderer is at large in England and the police are unable to catch the criminal, although they have used all of the scientific tricks and methods at their disposal, we feel defenseless, even though an ocean separates us.

The fact is that all emotions are subsidiaries of insecurity, which, in turn, happens to be self-preservation, the prime mover of *all* human conduct. Our emotions are aroused to the highest pitch whenever—in reality or imagination—our security is endangered.

No reason or logic governs emotion. Most of the time it is spontaneous. Without it life would be impossible. It is the

forerunner of evil or happy tidings and the invisible guardian not only of our well-being but, in the last analysis, of our
lives.

The specter of danger haunting people in creative literature reminds us of our own safety. Whatever happened to
others can happen to us. This is the reason then that even the
shadow of danger panics us and our emotions are instantly
aroused.

SURE-FIRE IDENTIFICATION

When a man, woman, or child is threatened by fire, flood,
earthquake, wild animals, loss, embarrassment, fear; when
there is hunger for love, food, companionship, vengeance;
when one is shy, orphaned, ill, abused, humiliated; when
charity, humility, kindness, loyalty, courage are displayed—
audiences will not fail to identify. And there are a million
other emotion-packed possibilities.

4

The Importance of Being Important

The importance of being important. Would it shock you if I stated that all writing, from its very beginning, grew from that root?

It is true! Read any play or story and you will find that whether it deals with love or hate, honor or dishonor, what lies behind it is the desire to be important!

"Desire" is a mild word for the strongest motivation there is, second only to "Self-Preservation."

I dare say that to be important is a part of self-preservation. It is certainly the force which moves a man to action even though he is well-fed and in no physical danger.

No writer can create a three-dimensional character without knowing why people act as they do.

Understanding the importance of being important helps us to understand how a human being, even the simplest, can so camouflage himself that only by accident or foresight can we detect behind the imposing façade a frightened mollusk.

The greatest mystery on earth is man. He looks so simple, so tractable, and actually is so complex. He says one thing and in the next instant shamelessly contradicts himself and, if you call him unreliable or unstable, he is mortally wounded.

He tells you, and believes it, that he is incapable of doing anything wrong—ever. He has the best of intentions. The blame must fall on the other fellow, who invariably commits all the blunders.

Don't you recognize this man? I am sure you must know at least one. He grows everywhere, like a weed. You don't? Too bad, because he is you and me, all of us—with a few exceptions. But those who admit that they too can be wrong sometimes are unnatural people, even mad. The general rule is that even if you or I made a mistake, it is really not our mistake; we rationalize until we've convinced ourselves that the blame must fall on the other fellow.

Why should this be so? Why must you or I be always blameless? Why must you or I be always right? Very simple. Because we are terribly insecure.

You may say that you are insecure, but that not everybody feels that way. I am sorry, my friend, but only mad people or idiots can live in such a happy nirvana that insecurity is nonexistent.

Insecurity is the basic law of existence. All human emotions and all actions, good or evil, without any exception, spring from this one eternal source. Without insecurity, there would be no progress. Life would stand still. Life would be impossible.

Security? Yes, there is such a thing, but it is so transient that one moment it's here and the next it's gone. You can't keep it long enough. You can't ever be bored with it, because the slightest flutter of dissonance makes it melt into thin air without a trace.

Motivation is endless—but still it can be simplified, if you accept the concept that insecurity is one of the most important and complex of all human emotions and conflicts.

Insecurity is as well disguised as neutrons and electrons are in that almost impregnable shell, the atom. Generally speaking, it cannot be recognized at first glance.

Still, insecurity is at the bottom of all human actions, be they good or evil. All cowardice or heroism, all human sacrifice happen because the authors of these deeds wish to annihilate the eternal, the indestructible menace of our life—insecurity.

There goes a man all puffed up. He plays the big shot, dressed to kill, big diamond pin in his necktie. He must be important. He is, and wants the whole world to see it.

Why? Importance is the first defense against insecurity. But there goes another man, a very well-known man indeed, a millionaire. And he looks like an ordinary working stiff. What does he hide? He is really very important. Why not show it? Do you know the answer? Of course you do. Everyone knows how rich, how influential, how powerful he is. He doesn't want to arouse more envy and hatred than there is already, so he prefers to hide his wealth and his shaky security behind a well-simulated simplicity.

Insecurity is versatile. It can hide in the most improbable places. Even loyalty, the most beautiful concept, is nothing but a hiding-place, a price for security; we think we're getting love in return. But security at best is a very unstable, a very unreliable friend.

Love, too, is a very good atom-bomb shelter in which to hide against insecurity. For our undying love we hope we can buy in return eternal love, which would spell security for us. But love, like everything else in life, is perishable. It changes with the passing of time and if you aren't careful, undying love may turn into just the opposite—hate—and death.

Let me see if this is true by examining a few case histories I personally know about.

A happily married man, the father of three beautiful children, loved by everyone, goes out one day and commits suicide. Why?

A charming young woman with a loving husband and a

little genius of a boy actually throws herself at any man who wants her. Promiscuity? No. Lack of love? No. Her husband is likely to commit suicide or murder if he discovers her infidelity; still, she has to go out with other men, even if the price be death. Why?

A rich man forges a signature on a check, is arrested, tried and sentenced to one year's imprisonment. No financial reason made him do this. Then why did he do it?

I can go on this way endlessly, but let me look more closely at these cases and see if my supposition that insecurity is the basis of all human emotion is true or false.

Importance is the first line of defense. It's good for the ego and for our health, too, but it can capture security, the dream of all dreams, for only a very short space of time. You see, your importance is a very unstable commodity. Many people envy it, and many try to undermine and destroy it.

Oh, there are many ways to make yourself important. Try humility, for instance. It works every time. Some men parade in humility as if it were a beautiful garment.

There is a very good reason for this. Great humility makes one important. Great sacrifice will do the same. It will raise you above the crowd. People feel that no price is too great for admiration, and many jeopardize their lives to achieve it.

The man who committed suicide in reality had good reasons to do away with himself. The autopsy showed that he had been hopelessly sick with cancer, but for the love of his family he had kept it a secret.

But people seldom commit suicide because of illness alone, even if that illness is a fatal one. People usually cling to their lives to the bitter end. What could have been another reason?

Financial difficulty would be a second cause and—perhaps this is the most important reason—under the surface he knew that his "loving wife" wasn't so loving after all and would not see him through a prolonged sickness. Only those people commit suicide who have lost the last shred of hope.

A candidate for suicide must have more than one reason to believe that all the claims holding him to life are gone—gone forever. So he dies, because he can't be important any more, and he is too humiliated to show himself in this pitiful and deplorable condition to those he loved. The only way out of this dilemma for him, he thinks, is death.

In death he expects to arouse compassion, tenderness, even pain in those he cares about. And at the price of his life he'll make himself once more, for the last time, important.

And now there is the young wife who throws herself at any man who wants her, thus courting murder and suicide. Why? It is a pitiful tale to tell. She feels that she, as a woman, is a total flop. Her figure, as she explains haltingly, never developed as it should have. She has very small breasts. But she's chic, good-looking and charming. What more can anyone ask?

Didn't her husband marry her? No, he didn't, she tells me.

"I went after him, courted him, pleased him. I gave myself to him as an inducement, played the virgin when I wasn't, flattered him, built up his ego, helped him in his business. Made myself indispensable—and now. . . ."

"And now that you're indispensable to him," I said, "what else do you want?"

"I want to be like other women. I die from sheer envy when I see a girl with a full bosom. The bosom is the beauty, the glory of a woman, a sign of fertility. . . ."

"You have a wonderful body. . . ."

"Men don't desire me as they do other women. I want to be desired . . . " she cried. "I know I am no good, going from one bed to another, but I'm looking for the assurance that I am every bit as desirable as any other woman."

"When you make a conquest, why aren't you satisfied?" I asked.

"How can I be?" she answered bitterly. "The men I give myself to are never the kind a woman can be proud of. They may just pity me . . . or perhaps I wooed them, instead of their wooing me. Oh God, I'm not a woman." And she cried and cried.

Would you call her a bad woman? No, not I. I wouldn't. She's just an unfortunate person, thrown into the arms of cruel and seemingly eternal insecurity.

I hasten to add that not all flat-chested women try to establish their femininity with an always new and exciting male, served to them at bedtime. But one thing is certain, and that is that anyone with a deficiency will try to compensate.

I mentioned before, and I'll do it over and over again, that there is no one who is wholly satisfied with himself. Ergo, we're all looking for some kind of compensation. The differences between people lie in the severity of their own shortcomings.

And the degree of satisfaction with ourselves will be determined by our physical make-up and our immediate environment. Hypersensitivity over the slightest disapproval usually springs from a weak body with a low physical resistance.

I am sure you know a few similar cases yourself. Of course you do. A big nose, or big feet or hands, or lack of hair, or too much hair, or a bad kidney, or varicose veins can make anyone the victim of the most insidious of diseases: fear. And fear is inseparable from insecurity.

I know a young girl who committed suicide because one of her ankles was thicker than the other and there was no money to finance an operation. She had no ambition and no other outlet for her imagination to work on. So that thick ankle apparently meant life and death to her. But let us never forget that no one ever commits suicide for one reason only. In this case the thick ankle was only the last, the very last straw.

Whether people know it or not, they constantly look for an outlet for their talents; they want to succeed, to better themselves, to be noticed, to be important. Great ambition is usually a compensation for some deficiency in the person. Most of the great men of the world became great for that very reason—because they felt there was something wrong with them.

Remember the man who forged the signature and let himself be jailed? I am sure you know now why he did such a stupid thing. Didn't he know what was going to happen to him if he was caught? Of course he did. He did it to be caught. Can you guess why he did it? Insecurity, yes. But will he be more secure in jail than out of it? Of course not.

I told you before, insecurity hides in the most impossible places. In this man's case he forged that signature deliberately, because his family looked on him as merely a walking meal ticket. He complained many times that nobody cared for him anymore. They laughed in his face and told him, "Of course we love you, Pop," and promptly forgot him again. Forging that signature was a trick to punish them and to shake them out of their complacency. He wanted to be noticed, he wanted to be the center of interest once more.

This man's action cannot be characterized as a stroke of genius. It simply indicated his mental and physical level. Another person in his place might have acquired some kind of a hobby. Another might have gone overboard for women. It all depends on the individual involved. I wish to emphasize over and over again that all human emotion and conflict originate from this one and only source—insecurity.

Fear is always humiliating, for it shows naked insecurity. To show insecurity is to strip man of his dignity. What is dignity? A camouflage for importance.

To show the lack of dignity is to court abuse. Such an exposed man, to cover his lost importance, starts to holler, to challenge, to abuse, to accuse, to show even bravery when, in reality, he is frightened to death.

The importance of being important is to hide fear, child of insecurity and mother of all human emotions.

To build a façade of importance is inborn as hunger is inborn.

5

The Shaping of a Character

Many of my students complain that although they have interesting characters in their minds, they don't know what to do with them. My advice is first of all to understand your characters. Be they despicable or admirable, find out (and write out) what made them what they are.

The exploration of a character, past and present, can be a fascinating piece of writing. The character outline, down on paper, can itself suggest a story or a play.

For instance, here is the outline of a jealous man.

A jealous man is usually an angry man, whether he knows it or not. I might go further and say that he is also prejudiced. This poor fellow would go to any length to rationalize and prove to himself, and to others, that his conduct is just and that it could not be different, even when it culminates in tragedy.

If you try to change his mind, you will find that he is the proverbial immovable object. What is wrong with him? Why should he be so adamant, so ready to die rather than to relinquish his jealousy? The answer is simple: he cannot change. His jealousy may subside for a time, but the old burning hate which underlies it is still there.

Let's call him Otto. Otto is going to kill his wife. Right

now, Otto is only seven years of age, and many years must pass before he becomes a man who is going to kill his wife, who is a woman of whom he has no conception as yet, no idea of how she looks, where she lives, or if she is yet alive!

What nerve! What audacity! What presumption on my part to play God! How can anyone prophesy years beforehand exactly what will happen to a man?

Ladies and gentlemen, what I am going to do with this man will not be a prophecy at all, but an act preordained. By whom? The answer is—by me! There have been men who killed their wives, but I have never met them. I do not know their backgrounds, their inherent characteristics. I do not know the myriads of seemingly insignificant episodes that helped to shape them.

Since, therefore, I have to create my own character who shall kill, I must assume the role of a personal God for this man. I shall shape him, then—and let him go! I shall watch as he stumbles, falls, gets up, kills, as in a Greek tragedy—if it is foreordained that he will kill.

Let me start at the beginning. Otto is an only child. He is at the moment not more than seven years old. His mother is a fine young woman of gentle ways. She is very sensitive about her slimness, although her husband married her in spite of it.

"Olga—are you asleep? For Heaven's sake—don't pretend! It is only half-past one in the morning. I couldn't help coming home late. Olga—say something! I just saw your light snap off as I put my key in the door."

She is abnormally jealous of her husband and would never fall asleep until he was home, but she is afraid to admit this. Olga cries at the slightest provocation. The great tragedy of her life is that her right leg is an infinitesimal degree shorter than her left leg. The fact is that in nine years of marriage Oscar has never noticed this defect. Olga, with infinite care,

THE SHAPING OF A CHARACTER

has succeeded in concealing what she considers a horrible disfigurement.

Her slimness also makes her fear that one day her husband will leave her for a well-stacked pin-up type. Her surreptitious glances in her husband's direction when they watch television never fail to detect aroused interest at the sight of vulgar, big-breasted females. She eats all the fattening foods without any success. Her fear of divorce made her decide to have a child, and little Otto, after her miserable pregnancy, became a living anchor for her marriage.

Little Otto, named for her recently deceased father, is as delicate as she, but he resembles Oscar, to her never-ending distress. She has a secret resentment against her husband. His eyes are so close together that sometimes he has an almost grotesque expression on his face. And little Otto has this same almost cross-eyed look that makes her despair.

Her husband is a good man—thoughtful, attentive—a lawyer with a good income and very respected in their community. But Olga would never have married him but for the shortness of one leg and her extreme slimness.

Slowly she became used to her husband's eyes and she could look at him without a shudder. She was very pleased that all her friends liked him and never mentioned his eyes as something of which to be ashamed.

Let me stop here and make a few remarks to writers. If I wish to establish that this child will become a murderer after he grows up, I have to stack the cards against him. The fact is that his tendency to murder started even before he was conceived. How did this happen? Olga feared to marry a normal man who might have a right to resent her lameness if he discovered it. Ergo, she felt it was necessary for her to marry a man who had some kind of physical defect.

After little Otto was born she felt that she should never have had a child. "Poor darling," she often sighed to the baby, "Miserable darling!" Resentment was in her heart and she felt terribly guilty for bringing Otto into the world. More than once she knelt near the child's crib, banging her head against the floor and crying hysterically.

But as the child grew, his charm and his wonderful, spontaneous laughter made her heart swell with pride. Otto was a little brute, with a wild imagination, so that all the fairy tales he heard from his mother he re-enacted without a flaw. Frequently she was astounded at the child's versatility. The misery started only when the child began to attend kindergarten, and then elementary school. The boys in his school called him "one-eyed Charlie." He fought them ferociously and often came home smeared with blood.

Now let me stop again and see what I have developed so far. I have a fear-ridden mother who is neurotic and jealous and who is convinced that all men, and all the gods, have conspired to make her suffer. She pities her son even more than herself. She has given Otto love in such abundance that he is almost suffocated by her outpouring of pity and tenderness. Overwhelming and burdening love for a person—lover, parent, child, or friend—is always a sign of weakness, the sign of a fear of loneliness and of dependency.

Olga's growing fear that her husband will eventually leave her for another woman makes her lose more weight, and now she looks almost transparent, with an unnaturally grayish pallor.

One day Olga's fear becomes a reality—her husband asks her for a divorce! After the first shock and hysteria, she becomes morbidly silent and withdrawn into herself. Otto, however, has been growing up slowly in the airless incubation of his mother's protective love. He knew no hostile wind until the boys mocked him.

He runs home from school after a miserable day and throws himself into his mother's arms for comfort. Olga thrusts him away and shrills, "You grotesque monster—you cross-eyed idiot, don't haunt me!"

There is no transition from his mother's protective love to the marrow-chilling blast of her hate. The delicate mechanism of his faith is shattered. He cannot trust his mother's love, so he cannot trust anything or anyone. The next day Olga is even more loving than in the past; two days later she is cursing all men and shouting at Otto if, indeed, she notices him at all. The pattern continues.

At the age of fifteen he attacks his mother with a large kitchen knife. "Just when I was kissing him!" the miserable woman cries. "He tore himself away, came back with a horrible carving knife to kill me!" Luckily he is restrained by neighbors who have heard her screams. They cannot understand how a quiet, obedient child could attempt such a hideous crime. But Otto by now is unbalanced. He is frightened of any demonstration of kindness from anyone because he suspects that under the smiling exterior must lie the inevitable rejection.

Otto has lost the capacity for trusting. He becomes a lonely man. He is always going out of his way to help the unfortunate, but he inevitably starts to run before the recipient of his kindness can express gratitude. He is afraid to make friends, for he expects today's friend to turn into tomorrow's enemy.

He is Otto the man, a chemical engineer, respected and admired by his colleagues but terribly lonely.

Now the writer must find a way to bring him into contact with Her, whom he is going to marry and eventually kill.

What kind of a woman would he marry, this man who distrusts those who flatter? She would have to be a strong and intelligent woman, with honesty her greatest virtue. She would have to hate and distrust all falsehood. He might be fascinated by such a woman. It would seem to be a perfect match.

They marry and, strangely enough, after many years of marriage she actually falls in love with her husband, and her devotion knows no bounds. Otto becomes fearfully disturbed about this very attitude. He fears treachery.

Now the stage is set for tragedy. We need only a spark, an incident, an unguarded moment in which she loses patience and says that she married him only for pity.

Here is where my suggestion for character must stop; the rest depends on your inventiveness and imagination as an individual writer.

Otto is likeable, but his dread of hypocrisy makes him hopelessly unhappy. What does he know about hypocrisy? Nothing. He has never allowed any human being to come near enough to commit this hideous crime against him. But as far as he is concerned, all smiles, all kindness, and especially all praise, are personal insults, an attempt to make him swallow feebly disguised treachery.

A protagonist like Otto must be made of material which cannot change under any circumstances. A protagonist, in order to achieve his purpose or goal, may bend, but change is out of the question.

The role of change is for the antagonist.*

The protagonist may go from determination to despair, or from determination to cruelty, as the antagonist stiffens against his onslaught. The protagonist is ready to be destroyed rather than give up. Then relentlessness must be established before the writer or dramatist puts a line down on paper.

We have seen why Otto is a jealous man, why mistrust cannot be eradicated from his mind. His is not sudden, spontaneous jealousy. I am speaking of that jealousy which is a

* For a full explanation of this point, read *The Art of Dramatic Writing*, by Lajos Egri (Simon & Schuster, New York, 1946).

deep-rooted affliction; this is the most virulent type and it must be inborn or acquired very early.

In considering the jealous person in general, we must be aware that he is inferior to those around him. He must realize that his own ability to progress is limited. To admit this limitation is shocking to him and this makes him bitter and jealous. He scrutinizes his adversaries more than an average man would do. He is always alert for the camouflage which hides the phoney. Whether he sees the real thing or not, he is quick to cry, "It is a fake!" He may become a crusader, a human bloodhound against all pretenders, and thus camouflage his own shortcomings.

Before jealousy there is suspicion; before suspicion, antagonism—the basis for growing hate. No one can be jealous without rancor.

There are dislikes, such as abhorrence, which are not jealousy. The writer must be aware of the difference between jealousy and other malignant outgrowths of emotion.

Practically all great men have some kind of physical or mental deficiency that they try to cover up, but when a man throws himself into the maelstrom of human experience and tries to prove with all his might that he is not only as good as his fellow-men but better, his drive is transformed into ambition. While jealousy is really sterile, revolving around its own axis, ambition is a movement arching into the future, eager to build. Even if ambition fails at the end it will be more constructive than the self-destroyer, jealousy.

An ambitious man is eager for honor, superiority, power, fame and wealth. Why? To cover up the inferiority which he is ashamed of. Inordinate ambition is the sign of greater than normal insecurity and the realization that the importance of being important is an absolute necessity for establishing his superiority over the common herd.

6

Improvisation

The other day I had a wild impulse to write about something, anything, without precisely knowing what. "Why plan?" I asked. "Why choose a worthy theme to write about? Why can't I be free as a bird and fly into the endless blue without a compass?" Fine, I will have fun. What shall I write about?

Funny, although I have decided not to worry about structure, concept, and all the difficulties a writer has to face, I am stumped at the very beginning. I must start with a *character*. Okay, I shall start with a character and let him go wherever he wishes. What kind shall I choose? I don't want any normal, everyday person. He should be someone I really don't know.

It will be an experiment. A holiday, so to speak. He will be . . . let me see . . . I shouldn't be too hasty. After all, I have to have some knowledge of the man with whom I want to go out for a lark. How about an artist? No. A flier? No, no. A banker? Of course not . . . A bum . . . a good-for-nothing pimp? But what shall I do with . . . wait a minute . . . I never knew a pimp. How can I set out with him? Wait a minute! I can question him. I will be his alter-ego and ask him such questions as only an alter-ego could ask . . . or answer.

44

I know a pimp must be an outlaw, a criminal, who has a crooked mind. His foresight has been damaged, or perhaps he never had any. But one thing is certain, this man must have a set of intimate characteristics possessed by no one else on this earth. In order to find out all about it, I have to become both him and his questioner who intends to live as a parasite himself. Let me show you what I have in mind:

Q. What do you think of your father, Victor?

A. He is an old drunkard with cauliflower ears, and I have no real witnesses that he is my old man.

Q. Let's suppose that he *is* your father—do you love him?

A. Not me. Any male animal can be a father. What's so wonderful about that?

Q. Why don't you love him?

A. Because I hate his guts. When I was in rompers, he used to kick me around and I still feel it in my head. He used to say to my old lady that I was as disgusting as a cockroach to him—and if she didn't get rid of me he would step on me one day and squash my dirty little head to a pulp.

Q. You couldn't remember *that!*

A. Maybe not, but it's true.

Q. How about your mother?

A. Ugh! My mother! She was the most disgusting female I've ever seen. Udders like a cow, hanging on her like two big empty bags which were supposed to drive a man crazy. I don't see how any man, including my drunken father, could go to bed with her. But somebody must have—because here I am!

Q. How about your sister?

A. She's a brood cow too—no brains!

Q. It seems that you think a great deal of yourself.

A. I am one of a kind.

Q. What kind?

A. I'm smart—I'm not going to kill myself working in a factory.

Q. How about an office?

A. It's no better. Day after day filled with the same routine.

Q. Did you ever try it?

A. Sure. It's all right for a dirty foreigner, who don't know any better.

Q. But my good man, how about all the Americans who work in such places?

A. They are stupid too; rich men don't slave.

Q. Not all men are born rich.

A. I know that! But the ones who don't work are. It was their dear old pappies who were the real McCoy. Born in the slums, they became the big-shot gangsters of their time, cutthroats who left a few cool millions for their brats, who can afford to go around preaching honesty. They can go to hell.

Q. How old are you?

A. Thirty.

Q. How do you earn your living?

A. I do a little job here and there.

Q. What kind of a job?

A. I said "job." The rest is my business.

Q. Okay, have it your way. Do you want to get married?

A. Why should I buy a cow when I can get milk for nothing?

Q. What do you think of women?

A. Lay 'em and leave 'em!

Q. How about other men. Do you trust them?

A. Many a time I've caught myself distrusting even *myself*.

Q. How come?

A. I make up my mind to do a certain thing, and at the last minute I get an idea that another way would be better.

Q. Was it?

A. Well, what I'm trying to say is that—if you can't trust yourself, how in hell can you trust anyone else?

Q. Do you think you're a genius?

A. I get along—don't you worry about that!

Q. But I *do* worry. I'm going to write about you, and I really want to know who you are.

A. You're inside me; you figure me out!

Q. Do you read books?

A. What for? They're full of malarkey; too much gab. A boy and a girl do a lot of talking, then they go to bed. With me it's different. I start out by going to bed with a broad, and after that there's nothing to gab about.

Q. So love is a very simple problem as far as you are concerned?

A. Yup.

Q. Do you ever think of your future?

A. What future? We live until we croak.

Q. How about your old age?

A. One of these days I'll either be knifed or shot, and my old-age problem will be solved.

Q. Why should anyone want to kill you?

A. Well, there are a lot of married broads who are bored, and willing to experiment, and if their old man finds out she is horsing around—he is ready to shoot to kill.

Q. Do you think he is justified?

A. Of course not!

Q. How about decency and loyalty?

A. Oh, come off it. . . .

Q. Of course *you* wouldn't know—forget it. Aren't you pimping for two girls?

A. Four.

Q. Aren't you ashamed of yourself?

A. Man! I didn't force them into their work. They came to me for help.

Q. You are selling human flesh?

A. Selling? I'm just protecting them.

Q. From what?

A. From other pimps—guys who would rob them!

Q. Aren't you?

A. I'm different. They give it to me. I'm just like a husband to them.

Q. Nice husband—live on prostitution!

A. Man! Just show me one goddamn man or woman who doesn't sell himself or herself to someone. We're all in the same boat. We're all prostitutes, one way or another, as I see it.

Q. Do you believe in God?

A. Sure.

Q. Aren't you ever afraid?

A. Why should I be? I'm just a small-timer—let the big bastards be afraid!

Q. You don't give a damn what people think of you?

A. Man! You said a mouthful! (Silence) Now—do you know me any better?

Q. You are completely unscrupulous. You have no moral standards and no respect for anyone. I wonder how you, or any human being, can live like that?

A. I manage.

Q. I see you do; but still, you are an animal in human form. Any man who cannot think of any other human being but himself does not deserve the distinction of being called a man.

A. Okay—stop beefing. What's the verdict? Can you use me in your story?

Q. I'm going to show you as an example of human degra-
   dation. You are a specimen of the lowest order, whose
   mind is ossified, and remains so. Are you insulted,
   Victor?

A. Hell, no. I take you as *you* are, Mister—you just don't
   know any better. You're a square, that's all. You think
   your own goddamn way, and anyone who doesn't think
   the same way, you call him an animal! I dig you, Man,
   I sure do! You know why? 'Cause *I'm* broad-minded.

Q. Victor, I'm going to ask you a very important question,
   so be very careful before you answer. Do you think you
   can change? I mean, to become more human?

A. What do you mean "more" human? I am human!

Q. I think that I am wasting my time. Your type will
   never change. I'm sure I know you quite well by now.
   One more thing, though. Of course you're having sexual relations with all of your four girls?

A. Of course. They're *my* girls—wouldn't *you* in my place?

Q. No comment, Victor, and no more questions.

A. Man! Don't be afraid of me. I knew you wouldn't. . . .
   Hey! Hey. . . . What's your rush? . . . Now why in hell
   did he have to bang that goddamn door so hard. I dig
   him, though—He's just a poor brainless cockroach!

Now I have never met a pimp or any other kind of criminal in my whole life. Victor lives only in my imagination. I
have only imagined that he would react as I think he should.
But there are many other Victors, and I take it for granted
that they too would act according to their own individual
characteristics. But that is enough about Victor. Now I will
merge this unscrupulous man with a woman. What kind of
female could or would be willing to love such a man? At this
moment that is a rhetorical question because I do not know
her yet. I am looking for a woman who is his exact opposite.

Since he is a crook, the best thing I can do is to find someone who has no conception of wickedness.

She should be an idealist, someone who is innocence incarnate; someone of unimpaired integrity. I have a name for her—Barbara Watson. Nothing special, just a name.

I see no reason for questioning this girl as I did Victor. She would be unable to say much if she is untouched by life, as I have imagined her to be. (Somewhere, deep in my memory, there is something stirring. I seem to remember knowing just such a girl but, as yet, I cannot recall where or when.)

Even if I find out all I want to know about this girl there will be a difficulty in bringing two such worlds-apart persons together. How will this be possible? How can a girl of nineteen or twenty be so innocent? How can she not have had contact with men? And if she has, how can she remain so completely naive, knowing nothing about human perversity? Perhaps she's come from a far-away place where visitors are rare and long-remembered. I hesitate. I do not know anything about such a place and I do not want to do extensive research now. I prefer a girl from familiar surroundings.

A girl . . . from familiar surroundings. . . . I have just the girl I want! She is a former student of mine who is very vivid in my memory. She fits perfectly into the story and will help Barbara Watson come to life.

I know my student is the only child of a happily-married couple, but many details of her early life are from my imagination. Her father sold used cars in a small, quickly-growing Texas town. Barbara had developed a very serious case of rheumatic fever at the age of twelve. For long, miserable years she was confined to her bed. She finished her schooling from her bed (unfortunately, so far all this is quite true). The doctors and specialists told her disconsolate parents that the child would be lucky to live to be thirty-five years old. (In truth, she lived to be exactly thirty-five.)

Barbara overheard the doctor's report. Her parents never knew this, so they were cheerful and confident in her presence, and promised her a long, happy life.

She read two or three books a day, many relating to natural phenomena and science. The doctors let her leave her bed when she was twenty. But a great tragedy—the death of both parents in an automobile accident—sent her back to bed with double pneumonia. Members of her church helped Barbara through her long and painful recuperation.

Her minister, Reverend Bert Hutchins, persuaded a mechanic who was a member of the congregation, and a friend of her father's, to take over the used-car business and share it fifty-fifty with Barbara.

She had no relatives except a great-aunt who lived in New York City. (As you see, I need this New York locale to bring Barbara into close proximity to Victor, the pimp.)

She wrote to this great-aunt and asked if she might come and live with her. The old lady agreed. Barbara arrived in New York within a few days of receiving the letter. The aunt, whom she had never seen, was old, wrinkled, and as unpleasant and set in her ways as they come. She was a widow who ran a cheap rooming-house in Greenwich Village. She welcomed Barbara with as much feeling as she could command, and gave her a dark little room on the lower floor, near her own.

Although Barbara ate with her aunt, she spent most of her time alone, reading science books from the library or watching television.

One evening, while her aunt was away, a fuse blew out in Barbara's section of the house. When she knocked on the door next to hers for assistance, a tall, blond, good-looking young man asked her what she wanted. (He was, of course, Victor the pimp.) Even though he decided she was not his dish, he went out and bought a fuse and soon the lights were on again. In appreciation Barbara invited him for coffee. He found her not only innocent, but disgustingly innocent about what most girls discover in their early teens.

But she too made a discovery. Victor, with all his poise and cheap witticisms, had never read a book in his life! They talked for several hours, and thereafter he came back day after day to hear Barbara's exciting little lectures about the cosmos and the immense galaxies of stars. She explained the earth's relationship to the sun as a life-giver, and the creator of all the other satellites, and the sun's juxtaposition in the cosmos to the earth's immediate family, The Milky Way.

Victor was astounded to hear so much knowledge coming from this naive girl with the shining, childlike face who sat quietly beside him.

Victor couldn't explain it, but he became aware of a strange feeling of confusion. He had always prided himself on his quick mind, his ready tongue, his penetrating points and his invariable rightness. In his simple mind, everything was simple. But Barbara somehow made everything different. He began to doubt that he was the wisest man in the world. He felt ashamed, ignorant, with a disturbing desire to know more.

He loved to sit and listen to her quiet, wonderfully sooth- ing voice. Once when she told him about light years, he asked in astonishment, "What in tarnation are they?" Barbara, with a silent joy, explained that light travels 186,000 miles per second and, by knowing this, you can figure out how far light travels in sixty seconds, in an hour, a day, a week, a month, or a year. Victor was spellbound.

On this same day, he went to the apartment of his four girlfriends and asked quite proudly what they knew about light years. The girls didn't know a thing about them and cared less. But Betsy, the blonde girl, told him he was very smart, and Arah, the brunette, told him he should be a pro- fessor.

Barbara lived for Victor's visits but her great-aunt didn't like the idea of their friendship. She warned Victor he had better let the girl alone, or else.

So Barbara went to his room, to tell her eager student about the discoveries and insights she had accumulated through her long illness. Victor was especially impressed with the constellations and the relationship of the moon to the tides of the ocean.

One day her great-aunt heard their voices and burst into Victor's room. She gave him a good thrashing with her cane and called him names that were strange and ugly in Barbara's ears. However, this attack didn't end their friendship. He invited her to the apartment of his four girlfriends. She happily accepted and he was delighted as he watched the girls listening to her stories of the majesty of the universe and the smallness of the atom. Arah, surprisingly enough, asked very sensible questions and Barbara answered them eagerly, with the devotion of a dedicated crusader. She had no conception of the girls' work, nor their first amusement at someone wrapped up in science to the exclusion of being a woman.

After a few visits to the apartment, Barbara noticed their little group began to grow. She became the Socrates of this strange group. To keep up with their questions, she went to the public libraries and museums, and read furiously to satisfy their growing interests.

After a while Barbara noticed that one girl or another would disappear into a back room with a strange man and then would hurry back, as if nothing had happened, eager to listen to the subject being discussed.

She asked Victor about it. Were they displeased with her talk, were they bored, or had she said something unpleasant to offend them? Victor was shocked by her unbelievable naiveté. Curious, he began to question her about her past, and slowly Barbara told him all about herself and her parents' violent death.

He was deeply shocked. Perhaps for the first time in his flippant life he felt real pity for a person. To him she was not a woman but a personality, who had given him something he had never dreamt about—a new world.

Sex was a cheap commodity in Victor's life. Therefore he respected Barbara without realizing it. Many times he was abashed by her and often he didn't know how to talk or behave in her presence.

Having heard her story and observed her frail appearance, he was sure she would die at thirty-five if not before. He didn't believe in angels but, to him, she was something out of this world, disturbing and unusual.

It was difficult to tell Barbara about the girls' profession. Victor had noticed, however, that when they went to the back room with a male visitor, they returned hastily, hurrying their unwilling guests in order to listen to the phenomena of creation.

The girls especially liked to hear about rain and snow, or the breathtaking production of a rainbow. Barbara warned them she was only an amateur in the field of science, and advised reading books from the library. However, they preferred to listen.

Victor was touched by Barbara's kindness. One day he began to make love to her. She pushed him away, and actually he was more relieved than offended. But he felt he owed something to this strange creature and decided to do something (he had no idea what, but something terribly big) for her. He wanted to show his appreciation for her kindness. If he had had the money, he would have taken her away to regain her health. He wanted to beat the ultimatum of the specialists who had decided she couldn't live past thirty-five. He would give her Life, instead of mink coats and jewelry! He was exhilarated by his glorious thoughts.

He decided he would get money for Barbara. He wasn't

sure how, but he knew he'd have to be very careful lest she be disappointed and angry with him should she find out about his plans.

From sheer pity, he made many tentative, slight advances toward her. She appreciated his kindness, she told him, but she couldn't believe he wanted her that way. He was hurt, then insistent. He did want her! At last she let him make love to her. It was the first time in his young life that he couldn't function as a man. This failure had a catastrophic effect on Victor's future life.

I had better stop the improvisation right here. I have reread the story and I am impressed that instinctively I have orchestrated the characters.

What did my improvisation prove? It proved, to me at least, that in any type of writing characters must be interdependent.

Without orchestration, the story or play will be colorless. Without unity of opposition, no story or play can exist at all.

I would compare a well-built story or play to a healthy person whose internal organs function smoothly, effortlessly. Improvisation would lead to exciting situations because you are working without any restraints. It is really fun. It should be fun. By the way, creation should never be a hard labor anyway. But play.

Victor's failure to function as a normal man foreshadows great change in his life. It is a foretaste of age, even impotence. His ambition will be fertilized by fear of ridicule. The story should focus on his ambition to build some kind of prestige, be it honorable or dishonorable. The turmoil in him is the agony of planning how to be important, even among the lowest.

7

Character Contradiction

Every motivation of man is a rich source for story material. I am very much interested whether man does or does not change.

"What a foolish statement," you will say. "Of course he does." But I have a sneaking suspicion there is something in man—in fact in every living thing on earth—that basically, fundamentally, does not change.

In this chapter I want to prove my contention.

Socrates, the wise old man of the past, discovered truth by the following method: First, he stated a proposition, then found a contradiction to it and corrected it in the light of this contradiction. Then he found a new contradiction and repeated the procedure. Thesis—antithesis—synthesis.

I think this is a splendid method to follow. First, I will present the accepted concept that man *does* change. This will be the thesis. I will do my best to present this concept as clearly as possible.

Then I shall *deny* that man changes. And this will be the antithesis. The rest will be the conclusion.

THE THESIS: *Man does change.*

A friend of mine, a fellow Hungarian, told me the following story.

"I must have been twelve years old. I was a tall, wiry boy, recklessly fighting with everyone, and I was not afraid of the Devil himself. One day, going home from school, I amused myself by ringing the doorbells in all the houses I passed. I listened with glee to the curses of men and women who ran to open their doors. It was fun. But next day came the payoff.

"A schoolmate, a shy, pale, introverted little fellow named Louis, whom I had protected many a time from bullies, reported me to the teacher, who was an old grouch. Teacher asked me if the accusation were true. I said yes. I was ordered to stay after school from four to six every afternoon for a whole week, and to write some stupid proverb five hundred times daily. It was a bitter blow to my pride.

"The very next day I promised my betrayer that as sure as I was alive, I would cripple him after graduation. Graduation was still many months away, but never for a moment did I forget my personal vendetta.

"Finally the day arrived. My whole class was aware of my plans and many gathered after the graduation to see the show. (Fortunately, parents didn't attend graduation at my school.) Almost half the class had assembled, and still there was no sign of Louis. I will never forget the conflicting emotions that churned in my stomach. Then suddenly I saw him! He shot forth from the swirling mob and ran like a frantic rabbit in fear of its life. I started after him. The boys trailed behind. I was gaining ground steadily when all of a sudden he dashed into a house and, with a loud bang, closed the door. There was I, outside looking in. The boys felt cheated and hollered to Louis to come out. "Don't be a coward," they yelled. But Louis had more sense. He knew what was good for him. There was silence in the house. The boys started to ring the bell. They banged on the large oak door. There was no movement. Time passed and the boys, robbed of their fun, slowly drifted away.

"I stood there alone. I could have gone too, but my pride wouldn't let me. "The little weasel will not escape so easily," I vowed.

"It must have been an hour before the heavy oak door opened and a tall, fat man looked out cautiously. When he saw me on the opposite side of the street he called, 'Go home, you. The circus is over. Go on home!' Then he turned and motioned to someone inside, and Louis came out. He stood close to the big man, his guardian angel.

" 'If you are hankering for a good beating, boy, come on over!' the man yelled at me. I didn't go over but took an especially sharp stone from my pocket, aimed at his ponderous stomach, and let it go. It hit the mark. The man cringed and cursed. He caught Louis by the scruff of the neck and dragged him inside, slamming the door behind them. I was glad. I was jubilant. Louis could see now that he could not escape.

"I prepared myself patiently for another long wait. But then the unexpected happened. The door slowly opened. I sprang to my feet, expecting to see the fat man coming at me with a shotgun in his hand.

"I looked and saw Louis—all alone. Without any hesitation he started toward me. I stiffened. He might have a knife, I thought, or at least a handful of pepper to throw in my eyes. I stepped back, frightened at first, but at the same time curious to see what he'd do. There was a craven fear on his face. He was visibly shaking. His hands hung helplessly at his sides, palms open. He was not hiding anything. As he came nearer, he slowed a bit. His face was thick with fright, a sunken yellow—like my grandfather's death mask had been a few weeks before as he lay in his coffin. I kept staring at Louis. There was a finality in his expression, a sort of courage. Not fright as I had thought. Even more than courage. Acceptance of death. At that time I did not know, psychologically speaking, where he had gotten the self-control to overcome his cowardice, his fear of physical combat. He stood quietly in front of me, and in his weak voice he said, 'All right, Martin. I am here. Kill me!'

"I looked at him hypnotized. I did not know what to say or do. 'I was wrong, Martin. Please forgive me.' I heard him without comprehension. I thought he might start to run, but he didn't. He just stood there, unafraid now—waiting, accepting whatever was to come. I felt helpless. All my anger started to melt within me and I knew that I could not hurt him. How in Heaven's name could I hit someone who would not defend himself? I couldn't have lifted an arm against him even if I had wanted to.

"In a way I was both disgusted and relieved at the same time. I turned and walked away without looking back."

In this story we have seen a shy person, a physical coward, seem to harden under terrific pressure like a diamond and become something that he was not before.

We cannot renounce the gratifying thought that the species to which we too belong can grow from bigotry to absolute clarity. True, the pattern of one's life is set in childhood, but the impact of the sizzling, red-hot present—not all the time, but some of the time—is so strong, so overwhelming, that the granite mold is softened somewhat and, at the end, perhaps dissolved. And lo and behold, there emerges an almost-new man, like the ancient phoenix.

Fear is one of the most potent emotions in man. Why not? After all, it concerns his very life. Can we ever eliminate fear? Yes! We can! More often than not, we are lulled into tranquility by good health and calm, peaceful living—so much so that when danger strikes we are actually unprepared and the result may even be annihilation. The point we are trying to make is that *fear* could evolve into *trust*.

It is a truism by now that jealousy is the result of an inferiority complex. Inferiority is fear, the fear of inadequacy. Can one check inferiority by praise? By success? The answer is —yes, one can. It depends upon the strength and duration of the praise and success, and if we respect those who started this golden cataract.

In fact, an inferiority complex can be dissolved to such an extent that a new process may start which could culminate in an obnoxious superiority complex. This metamorphosis of course is as unhealthy as the original inferiority complex.

The greedy person who has been conditioned to look after his own selfish interests will not care whether man or the whole world goes to hell. He will be deaf and blind until he reaches his goal, whatever that goal may be. The greedy one, lacking emotional security, concentrates on economic superiority. He knows that he cannot expect love or sympathy, so he decides to build respect, or even fear, toward himself. Fear and respect are good substitutes for love, and at the same time serve as measures to show how near he is to the summit of achievement, when at last his greediness is appeased. He is old and very tired, but not tired enough. A new kind of greediness takes ferocious possession of him. Now he is greedy for respectability, for importance, for—immortality.

How can a heartless and cruel man become respectable, and even immortal? This is the simplest thing in the world— if you have enough money. He was cruel and uncommunicative before, but now he loves to pose as the great humanitarian. He knows quite well that in ten, fifty, or a hundred years, no one will remember the ugly, inhuman and vicious side of his nature. He knows as a certainty that his name will be emblazoned on many noble institutions, and that everyone will think of the wonderful, magnificent Mr. Joe Greedy only as a kind and shining example to his fellow man.

So he changes, and we are all going to change for better or worse, in spite of ourselves, because Nature is explicitly against standing still. . . .

Motivation? The same old story—self-gratification. But if humility helps us to create *sympathy*, or *importance*, we will put on the robe of humility and parade around in it as if humility were giving us the greatest joy in life.

The above would seem to prove that human beings do change. This is the first step according to the dialectical approach. Now I will try to negate, or contradict, all I have said.

I have stated the thesis—people *do* change. Now I will proceed with

THE ANTITHESIS: *People do not change.*

Who is a liar? Anyone who willfully misrepresents, shields, or hides a fact. The liar covers up; he cheats. But why should he lie? A lie may grow out of fear, or anxiety, desire for gain, for revenge, for fun, momentary glory, fame, or fortune, or simply out of a desire to create the illusion of being important.

Whatever the reason for lying, the end product is calculated gain.

A liar may wish to escape from an intolerable situation, or to help others to escape, or to conceal bad or disturbing news from others. Whatever its purpose, in the last analysis a lie conceals the fact of a present or impending event.

A lie then is to conceal. One might hide truth for a time, or even indefinitely, because to reveal it at present would be too disturbing or even catastrophic.

A lie may cover a desire to covet property or a woman or to conceal a sacrifice. It has many facets, and every one of them represents something different.

I am going to introduce you to a very nice gentleman who, unfortunately, is known for his bad habit of lying. Most people tell a lie once in a while, but our man is an inveterate liar. He exaggerates and hides behind falsehood even when there seems to be no apparent reason. But of course there are reasons—many of them, not just one—for this man's compulsive lying. He was an orphan, grew up in foster homes where, for the slightest infringement of the rules, he was slapped or beaten. Later his exaggeration—a tempered lying—was a great help in his profession. He became addicted.

This addiction did not prevent him from marrying and having children, or even from being happy. He philandered a bit, just as many men who aren't liars do. (A man who lies about philandering isn't necessarily a habitual liar.) But our liar-philanderer often forgot to be discreet, and in due time his wife became jealous. He tried to lie his way out of a bad situation, but his wife was no fool. She became accustomed to his lies. They quarreled, then separated.

Our man lived with another woman for a time, but he couldn't forget his wife. He started to woo her again. He promised by heaven and earth to be faithful from then on. His wife relented on one condition. If she ever caught him telling even a white lie, out he'd go! He accepted—swore off lying. But he found that not being able to exaggerate created in him a choking sensation. He felt miserable. He lost interest in his interest. Life became drab, intolerable, and the old habit slowly reasserted itself. Once in a while he caught himself telling some tiny, snow-white lie and afterwards he felt a prick of conscience. But like a drug addict, he must have a shot in the arm. He simply must lie!

Every lie must have some kind of base, a foundation, no matter how shaky, on which the liar can build. A fragment of a remark, a part of a piece of gossip is sufficient.

To build a good, enduring lie requires imagination. A believable lie is really a creation. The author—I mean the liar—should be proud of it! But I don't think a liar consciously creates his lies. They are impulsive. He hears a rumor. His mind reacts as does a seismograph to an earth tremor. He reacts almost without thinking. Now he feels bouncy again. He is full of energy, and in his element. Life is worth living!

Unfortunately for our liar, his new lies created a slow reverberation which grew in volume and eventually reached his wife. She in turn was ashamed, then outraged. Recrimination followed. He denied everything. But his wife remained adamant.

The writer can continue to follow this man through all the emotions a human being is likely to experience. He might change from an amiable, understanding husband into a ferocious and jealous husband. But whatever shape he takes, he will still be fundamentally the same. He will still be a liar. A brooding liar perhaps, *terrorized into silence*. The fact is, any changes that occur in this man will be only on the surface. The compulsion to lie may be buried, but it will still be alive. Because to him lying is the only means by which he can express himself.

Yes, a man does seem to change under pressure. But underneath, in the subterranean recesses of the mind, ambition, or whatever else he thinks is important, breathes as fiercely as before. His goal, under any circumstances, is the drive, the urge to remain alive. This never changes.

I happen to know a gentle old lady, a spinster, who belongs to a small Presbyterian congregation. Miss K. has no family. She lives alone, and all her free time is spent near or in the church, helping with every phase of its work. She should be the most beloved person alive, but unfortunately there are men on the Executive Board who would rather see her dead.

What could this innocent old lady have done to arouse the collective ire of such prominent persons as the druggist, the lawyer, the banker, the merchant, and the other members of the Executive Board of the church?

Miss K. is a bookkeeper in a paperbox factory. She earns a modest salary. But almost fifty percent of it goes every week to help out the impoverished budget of her congregation.

Since it is the established custom to announce in the

church's monthly bulletin the name of each contributor and the amount contributed, Miss K. is a source of unending irritation for the well-established people in the church. The tremendous disproportion between the old lady's offering and their own is embarrassing. "We cannot afford to contribute so much," they wail among themselves. "After all, we have many other expenses." But shamefacedly they are forced to give more than they would like to. The old lady learns about the rumbling, but she goes along as before as if it were of no concern to her. And horror of all horrors, suddenly she doubles her contribution. It is incredible! Staggering! It is too much to bear. The subject is brought up at the next church meeting. Where does she get the money? How can she afford to give so much?

She smiles sweetly and says she trusts in God, who provides for the humble. Then she walks away from the meeting. A few weeks later comes the real shock. Miss K. is arrested for stealing. The local papers headline the event. The humiliated bigwigs cackle happily. "That old witch! She is a good-for-nothing thief after all. Thank goodness we are rid of her at last!" They are sure she will never have the nerve to show her face again.

There is a trial. All the important people make it their business to attend. No doubt they want to gloat. This insignificant old woman with her mania for self-sacrifice had shamed them, and forced them into giving more and more, until it really hurt.

At church meetings she had reminded them quite often, with her sweet trembling voice, "Your Lord God needs much more than just lip service!"

"It is dangerous to argue with the old witch," they had agreed.

And now, here at the trial, they get another shock. Miss K. frankly admits she has been stealing for the glory of God!

When the judge asks her to clarify her statement, she proceeds to explain only too well that the church is in such a dilapidated condition that it is an absolute disgrace! She has given almost eighty percent of her weekly wages, but this never seems to be enough. She has been on the verge of starvation, without any sign of help in sight. Of course, she hurriedly explains, no one asked her to go hungry, but perhaps that is why she was prompted, in good conscience, to steal.

Bit by bit, she had pilfered $637.30 from the cash box. Not a penny more! And she gave it all to the Reverend to make the proper arrangements to renovate the church.

The Reverend then testifies that Miss K. did give him that amount. He explains that she had consulted carpenters, painters, and other artisans about the work. Actually, the work would have cost more than $2,000, but the God-fearing members of the congregation had agreed to donate their work gratis if the church would pay for the materials.

Confusion breaks out in the courtroom. Such sacrifice and devotion moves everyone. Even the representative from the paperbox company for which Miss K. works is melted by the emotional impact of the moment. He declares in a ringing voice that his company is withdrawing charges against her. However, she refuses to accept her employer's generous offer. She has sinned, she declares self-righteously, so she must be punished.

The judge understands this faithful stalwart of the Faith and promptly sentences her to six months of hard labor. Then, with a knowing smile, he quickly announces that the sentence is suspended! There is spontaneous applause in the court. The judge assures the blushing culprit that his leniency is based on his belief that the circumstances will not arise again. Miss K. promises that it will never happen again. That is, until . . .

"Until, nothing!" cries one of the members of her church.

A spokesman says, indignantly and sternly, "Sister K., from now on if the church needs anything, you must come first to the Executive Board for help. And I promise that if your complaint is legitimate and the situation warrants action, it will be taken care of sympathetically to the best of our ability."

People say the age of miracles is not over. This must be so, because before the court clears, the members of the Board stand up one by one and pledge the repayment of the $637.30 that Miss K. has stolen. The trial is closed on this note of beautiful brotherly love.

Who is Miss K.? Just a plain, poorly paid bookkeeper with no family, who has dedicated her life to God and the Church. She is known as a tireless worker, not for herself but for her fellow man. She seems selfless, without desire for earthly goods. What then is her motivation? As far as anyone could see, her only ambition on earth is to worship God and to demonstrate her happiness in serving God and his Son Jesus.

She has succeeded in proving this, but will she be satisfied now? Never! Rather than rest on her laurels, her glorious triumph will give her more courage than ever. She will demand more and larger sacrifices from others until the inevitable happens. She will be rejected by the very church she is trying to help, and she will find herself an outcast, branded as a perpetual troublemaker!

Miss K. seemed to change from pole to pole. No one can travel further than she did—from saintliness to crime. But the change was only on the surface. The granite determination and obsessive drive to strengthen her position before God never changed. Fundamentally, she never ceased to drive with increasing vigor toward the only goal she knew: to be important.

And now, here comes a really strange man. He is a writer, the father of three beautiful children, who, by his own admission, will never create any excitement in the world of writing. But this man, who is no genius and has no desire to become one, has justified his existence in a most bizarre way in order to perpetuate his own immortality.

If his bill in a restaurant comes to a dollar, he invariably leaves at least an equal amount as a tip. (It's true, I saw him.) He often tips cab drivers up to three times the actual fare. When I asked what compels him to be so generous when he can hardly afford it, he laughed and said, "I wish you could have seen the look on that cabbie's face when I gave him a $3.50 tip on a $2.00 ride!"

"You are a show-off, my friend," I said. "Do you think waiters and taxi drivers are impressed by that sort of thing? They know the biggest tippers are usually the poorest."

He assured me he knew all this. His further explanation was really something new. "Whether the waiters or the cab drivers think I'm a fool, a schmoo, or a show-off means nothing to me. I know darn well that not a single one of them will ever forget me! In fact, because of me, they may be courteous to innumerable bastards like myself in the hope that each will turn out to be as generous as I was! You see, my friend," he added, "to me, a good deed lives on and works some silent magic in the human mind."

"Very interesting," I remarked. "Then have you dedicated yourself to being a dispenser of goodwill among men?"

"Yes," he said eagerly. "But nothing compares with what I receive in return. The shocked and bewildered thank-you's constantly ring in my ears and I feel a joy so intense that I can hardly describe it."

"Interesting," I said. "I am sure that you have something there and, considering the return, the price is dirt cheap."

My writer friend was always considered to be an honest man, but lately he has begun to plagiarize. To plagiarize is dishonest. (Shakespeare did the same—but he was a genius!)

This once cheerful man has now become somber. Even his young, jovial face has hardened. Only the small smile-wrinkles around his childish brown eyes remind me that in the past he was addicted to laughter.

Only one thing from the past remains constant: his insane drive to be generous, to be important.

THE SYNTHESIS: In the thesis I stated the proposition that everything changes; only change is eternal. The antithesis was an attempt to contradict this statement—and to show that although man does change, the ever-present desire is to be important, to remain alive. The "Life Urge" is changeless to the very end.

I do not intend to talk about those who commit suicide. But I might point out that even suicide is the final attempt to be important when, in reality, only hopelessness remains.

Louis, the boy, the little coward, unflinchingly faced a crisis when there was no other way out. The reason—he hoped to escape a cruel beating, even injury. His cowardice, his original character, made him appear heroic when basically he remained what he was—a coward who was afraid to fight. This flight from a fight sprang from fear, and later, his submission sprang from the same course. He wanted to escape punishment.

Miss K. obviously never changed.

The liar was terrorized at first, then changed color. But he provoked crisis after crisis with his constant compulsion to lie. He remained true to his own character throughout.

The writer used over-generosity to become important. He became dishonest to satisfy the same need!

The greedy man remained greedy from the beginning to the bitter end. Once his insane drive for power was satisfied, he altered his methods and became generous in order to achieve a more enduring importance—his original ambition.

Yes, there is change.

A dishonest man under pressure can be forced to do the impossible—to become honest. The honest man, to whom honesty is the breath of life, with horror will realize that under certain circumstances he could become dishonest. The man who swears to be the most loyal person on earth can become the most disloyal. The unreliable, dishonorable man could sacrifice his life to fulfill a sacred promise.

How can we understand all these strange and contradictory statements?

Let us admit that without change life would be impossible *and we change in order to survive.*

In nature, animals, even insects, take on a false coloration in the struggle for survival. It is a necessity for man, too, to do the same. But once man has lost his capacity to change color, to blend into his natural habitat, he is forced to use his wits instead, in order to camouflage his attitudes toward his fellow men and secure his safety and his life.

To love or hate or be jealous is only part of characterization. A character might become honest, dishonest, a liar, a blackmailer, might even commit murder, and all for one basic purpose—to strengthen his position in life and his security; all the endless chameleon-like changes for one reason only—to remain alive, to be secure, to be happy and, most of all, *to be important!*

8

Forging the Unbreakable Bond

Let us suppose that you want to write about a day-dreamer, a person who feels that the world owes him a living, or one who believes that if he only were given the chance to become a lawyer, an inventor, or anything of importance under the sun, he could startle the world. He has unlimited confidence in himself, only he doesn't do anything about materializing his dreams. He only talks about them. A character of this sort makes fabulous story material. Daydreaming is a universal pastime for all of us.

If this sort of character is worth writing about, how shall we begin to write his story?

The right way to start any story is to engage your central character in conflict. You might ask, why conflict? For the simple reason that a character, any character, even you or I, will in conflict reveal himself in the shortest possible time.

It is always advisable to have opposites facing each other, in all types of writing, if you want to establish conflict from the very beginning.

These opposite characters should be militant, of course. Without militant opposition there would be no conflict. Conflict is life; a static situation is death. In nature there is no static state. From the invisible atom up to the stars, some million light years away, a constant struggle goes on. This struggle has been going on from the beginning of time and will last through all eternity. Don't think that only man dies. The stars perish the same way up in the far distance as man does on earth.

Matching different kinds of people against one another is called orchestration. This is vitally important in good writing.

An optimist might be opposed by a pessimist. They are exact opposites, and if both of them are militant, conflict will be inevitable. For the same reason, it is good to pit an honest man against a dishonest man; a spendthrift against a penny-pincher; a happy-go-lucky person against a morbid individual. The difference will show up like a white dot on a black canvas, or a wart on the face. Religious fanatics are best contrasted with militant atheists. A meticulous person should be contrasted with one who is completely disorganized.

If you happen to use two characters of the same kind, you must orchestrate them against one or two individuals who are the opposite of your first two. For example, two immoral people against one or more highly moral people.

Just imagine what would happen if two zealots like a dreamer and a realist were locked in an unbreakable bond, both pitilessly militant, believing 100 percent that their philosophy of life and approach to life are the only ones that are sound and logical.

If for any reason one of these combatants becomes tolerant of the other's weakness, the story dies stillborn. With a tolerant antagonist you might write a very colorful character study, but never a story where the reader's interest is held to the very end.

A realist thinks of a dreamer as one who commits the blackest of sins, while a dreamer thinks of a realist as a useless fool who doesn't deserve to live.

Now, if you have two characters as opposed to each other as a daydreamer and a realist, you have the foundation for a very good story. But before you go any further, you should find out why one cannot walk out on the other while the conflict is still on.

Suppose that the daydreamer and the realist are married. The man is a dreamer, the woman the realist.

My example need not be the same as yours. My outlook on life naturally differs from yours, the same as all human beings more or less differ from each other. The important thing to remember is that there must be two perfectly orchestrated characters who are hellbent to oppose or perhaps even destroy each other if necessary.

I am going to give you my version of an unbreakable bond between these two people.

The woman, in their courting days, was very much impressed with the man's idealistic outlook on life. It sounded romantic, colorful, and exciting. She was overcome by the eloquent plans this man made for the future. She didn't know then that this man's ability lay only in the planning.

The woman, who is the realist, overlooked at that time the fact that a portion of ice cream can be refreshing, but ice cream eaten several times a day for the rest of her life could become sickening.

Why didn't this woman, a realist, see the man's obvious shortcomings? She was thirty-five years old, very lonely and very frightened. She worried and wondered if she'd ever meet the right man who would want to marry her. She was a simple person with a conservative family background and one disastrous love affair behind her. After that sad episode she became frightened of men, in fact so lonely and hopeless that for a while she was on the verge of committing suicide. She had a little money in the bank to live on, a two-family home left her by her parents, and she was employed in a lawyer's office.

When the dreamer came along, she was overwhelmed by the presence of a good-looking male. The dreamer, on the other hand, was very much impressed by her devotion, understanding, and—let's be frank about it—her generous financial assistance to him. He hadn't any qualms about taking money from a woman because he was positive that he was going to become a very great author in a short time, like Hemingway or Dreiser, for instance. Then he would repay her a thousandfold for what she'd done for him.

Yes, the dreamer was an unsuccessful writer. A few of his character sketches had been published by small art magazines, which gave him a grand feeling of importance but no money whatsoever.

So they were married. At the beginning she needed him and hoped that everything would turn out for the best. The dreamer followed the same line of thought. The woman, being a realist, remained on her job. He worked on his great novel . . . when he wasn't talking about it to his friends. The tragedy was that he talked more than he worked. When the glory of newness wore thin, trouble started.

Let me give you my version of how conflict grew between these two.

Which do you think would start the trouble between them? I can assure you it wouldn't be the dreamer, because he desperately needed peace and help.

The woman, on the other hand, became increasingly impatient with her husband's tardiness, idleness, arrogance, and bragging. The worst blow to his vanity came when she would call him a braggart. She called him everything under the sun when she became angry with him, but nothing hurt him as much as being called a braggart. He would sulk for weeks at a time but, since he liked to eat, he usually apologized with great humility and promised to turn over a new leaf.

After five years of this, he began to realize that he had better do something to re-establish his wife's confidence in him. He couldn't help but notice that her restlessness and impatience were growing, and he was frightened lest she withdraw her support, without which he could never finish his life's work, the great American novel.

She, on the other hand, hated to throw out this useless bum for the simple reason that she woefully remembered her terrible loneliness before she married him. Also, she still believed that he might settle down and write a book which would make a fortune. Why not? It had happened to others. Why shouldn't it happen to him? Such reasoning as this, of course, was born of sheer desperation and not realism.

The unbreakable bond was thus forged from the dependence of these two people on one another.

The conflict, the real crisis of their life together, began when the dreamer came home one day with a sure-fire proposition. He had the chance of a lifetime, he said, to buy himself a half-partnership in a small advertising agency. The price was so trifling—laughable, he added—only a paltry ten thousand dollars. Her answer was such a vehement "No" that it started a fight which lasted for weeks.

At last he packed up his belongings, the little he had, and was ready to leave. It looked as if he meant it this time. His desperation blinded him to the fact that he really couldn't go anywhere because without her support he would be lost. In the end she grudgingly gave in to him, fearful of being lonely. The job didn't last long with him, and in a short time everything they had was gone.

Luckily she was still working, but the loss of her money made her more insecure and more frightened than ever before. She became sick, mentally and physically, and was in constant fear that he would leave her, for now there was nothing to hold him. It was a nightmarish, dreadful existence for her.

She began to cater to his wishes. She became more amiable,

more co-operative, and more affectionate to him. The dreamer, in a corresponding degree, became more hostile and more cruel to her. Confident now that she would never kick him out, he started to play around with other women.

The end? It will depend on what you wish to prove. What kind of premise do you want to formulate? Daydreaming leads to divorce? Or daydreaming leads to murder! He might murder his wife because she advertised his utter selfishness, cruelty, and dishonesty. She created scandal after scandal in public and deliberately went out of her way to humiliate him. She made his life so miserable that this worm, the man who had never done anything positive in his life, became so aroused that in a moment of hysterical fury he killed her.

You might have another premise for the same story: Daydreaming leads to success and happiness. It is possible, you know! At the last minute, before the last straw breaks the camel's back, something happens. The daydreamer's book is sold and it is a great success.

But if you formulate such an ending, daydreaming won't be the right premise for your story. You should change it to "Perserverance leads to success and happiness." A person with dogged determination and absolute faith in his own strength and ability sometimes looks dangerously like a daydreamer, especially if success eludes him for a long time.

There is a great difference between a daydreamer and a perservering man because, whereas the daydreamer dreams, the perservering man is a "doer," besides being a visionary. The unity of opposites between your characters, the unbreakable bond, makes any story possible. Out of this unity grows your story. The premise is a microscopic form of the story itself.

You might write an outline as I did now and ask yourself what you really want to say. Formulate a premise and start your story at a crisis which will be the turning point in your character's life.

The above story has grown out of character and orchestration. A daydreamer pitched against a realist, both of them militant and intolerant of each other's beliefs.

Another man might be a music lover who meets a young lady who loves music too. The difference between the two is that whereas the man makes music an obsession, the girl's appreciation is just moderate, normal, and nothing more. At the beginning, their infatuation and their various common interests will effectively obscure the real issue, which will grow into such fearful proportions later that serious complications will result.

This story too can start from orchestration. Find out why they can't run away from each other in the middle of their struggle—formulate a premise and you are ready to write your story.

Let me repeat: There is rich material for a story if two militant and entirely different types of characters are bound together in an unbreakable union; and, as they struggle to break their bonds, they will naturally generate rising conflict in the process.

Here are a few examples of perfect orchestration and the birth of a story:

Sensitive—Insensitive
Cheerful—Morbid
Vulgar—Spiritual

Take any one character and find his opposite, figure out why they can't separate, although that is the very thing they desperately wish to do, and you have a story.

Man has nothing more precious to defend than his self-declared importance, and he will defend it with his last breath.

9

Where Do Writers Get Their Ideas?

People wonder where writers get their ideas. Must they first experience what they write? Do they really rush wildly around looking for story ideas?

Good writers look for "characters," because ideas grow as freely from characters as apples from apple trees.

Every character grows not one but many fresh, unique, writeable stories.

Writers who want to write good stories or plays must know their characters better than they know themselves. Better—because most of the time we are unaware of the motivating forces within us.

Strange but true, it is easier to create a living, three-dimensional character than an unreal, one-dimensional character.

No miracle involved.

Let's suppose we know a person who is 100 percent charming and loved by everyone. Such a person needs only one insignificant trait to become disagreeable and hateful.

Let's say this person is a young lady. She's as charming as I mentioned, but I'm giving her one disagreeable trait—she is trusting.

But what's wrong with trusting? Nothing, if used in moderation.

Everyone is trusting once in a while, but this character is trusting twenty-four hours a day! She's a sitting duck for swindlers. And worse, since she cannot be distrustful, she might drag you into serious trouble, like blackmail, lawsuits, divorce—even murder. This one uncontrollable trait in her obliterates all that is admirable.

She cannot change.

Iago in *Othello* never changed. The mother in *The Silver Cord* never changed. The junkman in *Born Yesterday* never changed. Tartuffe never changed. And leading characters in all great plays, great movies, great novels, great stories, never change. They cannot.

If you have an unbending character, he will create his own story. Not your story, not mine, but his own, because he cannot do anything but be himself. Is he strong? He does not want to impress or show strength to frighten the weak. He simply wants to be left alone and be himself. As he cannot change the color of his eyes, he cannot change his outlook, his character, even if his life depended on it.

To find original stories, the rulers of the airways and their long-suffering writers need only pick one individual with an outstanding trait from among their acquaintances. One alone can provide story material for a dozen series.

The following characters will generate their own stories. *They could embody all virtues in existence,* plus the one trait which makes them lovable or intolerable to live with. And why should such people generate a story? Because they totally possess one trait—one trait which is 100 percent. A compulsive trait.

Here are a few:

ANALYTICAL: He is normal, only compulsively analytical.

He figures out reasons for your every movement, even if you haven't any.

CONFORMIST: She is a nice, peaceful person but she'd rather die than do anything out of the ordinary. Pair her off with a non-conformist who is militant, and watch how the sparks fly.

HYPERSENSITIVE: Orchestrate him with a crude showgirl. And remember, he'll be sensitive the rest of his life.

INFALLIBLE: What a horror to live with a person who is always right!

MATERIALIST: Pit him with an idealist. Do you hear him cry out when the idealist praises a sunset, "What do you get out of it?"

HYPOCHONDRIAC: Orchestrate him with a health fiend who looks at sickness as the greatest and the most unforgivable sin on earth.

IMMACULATE: Opposed to a sloppy person.

Let me remind you once more, the people possessing these compulsive traits should be bound together with an unbreakable bond to their opposite. Now, if you can figure out how to break the unbreakable bond between them, the struggle for liberation will make your story or play.

OVER-GENEROUS	SPENDTHRIFT
OPPORTUNISTIC	SCRUPULOUS
OPTIMISTIC	STOICAL
OBSCENE	SNOBBISH
PESSIMISTIC	FRUGAL
PERFECTIONISTIC	FLIGHTY
PERVERTED	GREEDY
SELF-RIGHTEOUS	GULLIBLE
RUTHLESSLY AMBITIOUS	SHIFTLESS
SENSUOUS	TIMID
DISTRUSTFUL	EXHIBITIONISTIC
EXTROVERTED	EXTRAVAGANT

SKEPTICAL	VINDICTIVE
TREACHEROUS	WASTEFUL
TRUSTING	EXACTING
UNSCRUPULOUS	CONNIVING
VAIN	EGOTISTICAL
VULGAR	FICKLE
VISIONARY	SYSTEMATIC

It is a must that a writer present a character—any character —as an individual. Even the Devil deserves his due. *No character is all black or all white.* A tantalizing revelation occurs when an apparently decent and reliable human being exposes himself as an unreliable gambler without conscience or foresight, jeopardizing the life of the man who trusted him implicitly.

Now let's reverse the procedure.

A character is despicable—unwholesome and treacherous. You wouldn't want to live on the same continent with him. He is almost intolerably black but he has one singular weakness which makes him human. He is afraid to grow old. Not afraid to die, mind you, but afraid to grow old. This man is cruel to all with whom he deals, except old people. He goes out of his way to treat them with gentleness. Strangers seeing this man with old people will consider him an admirable person. On the other hand, those who know him would never believe him capable of a single decent act, if his life depended on it.

The touchstone of great writing is to know your character and expose him in as many angles as possible. This can be done only if the writer knows the character's background, his inherited characteristics, his ambitions, his hatreds, his loves, his heroes, all the little and big episodes in his life which could throw a searchlight on the man as a whole.

WRITER: Call me a blockhead or a man without imagination, I don't care. But after all this explanation, I still

don't know how to create conflict. I know my protagonist backward and forward and yet my characters
refuse to move. What's wrong with me?

ADVISOR: Do you have an unbreakable bond between the
protagonist and antagonist?

WRITER: I have, but it does no good.

ADVISOR: Do you know the premise, the goal of your protagonist?

WRITER: Of course I do. I am sure something is missing but,
for the life of me, I can't put my finger on what.

ADVISOR: Read the following stories and I think you will
know how to activate your characters.

These stories and scattered suggestions have no structural
connection with each other. The origin of every character
remains to be explored. The purpose of these stories is to
show the inherent story possibilities in them.

THE WOOLWORTH TYPE

One word describes him—Tightwad! He's a young Scrooge,
strong and energetic, with money in the bank. Nevertheless,
he is so frightened about his future financial security that
spending money even for basic necessities makes him feel ill.
But he is human and he wants to fall in love and marry.

He finds a woman who is mad about him. She apparently
approves of his attitudes and aspirations. He assumes they are
soul-mates, never dreaming she would pretend to agree with
almost anyone who promised to slip a wedding band on her
finger. Actually, she marries young Scrooge fully intending to
change his penny-pinching ways.

She begins to suspect her plan will never succeed when her
husband refuses to spend money for the contraceptive she
requests. She becomes pregnant. Tightwad has morning sickness every time he allows himself to think of the mountain of
doctor and hospital bills ahead, not to mention the expense

of having another mouth to feed. He wonders if he should insist that his wife have an abortion before it is too late.

While he is still comparing costs, his wife is admitted to the Maternity Ward. Triplets! He is outraged. The inconsideration of the female race! Divorce. That is the answer. But after his lawyer advises him of alimony payments he reconsiders. It is far too expensive! He agrees to stay with his wife and family. "But we simply can't afford the luxury of marital relations," he warns his beautiful wife.

Eventually, however, the Hungry Beast in the human side of young Scrooge gets the best of him. His wife, knowing the strength of her position at last, refuses him on the grounds of economy. She urges him to visit another woman. Spending the money outside the family seems outrageous to him. She holds her ground, and finally, the thrifty young husband can hold his no longer. He agrees to pay her for their nightly extracurricular activities. She costs a little more than the free-lancers but she is good-looking. Anyway, there is always the possibility she might in some way spend the money on him. (She doesn't, though. The last time I saw her she was wearing a new mink stole.)

A cheap character offers endless possibilities for a farce. A crystalized character is the source of more ideas than you can use in years!

The Perfectionist

He knows precisely what he wants, and he's sure he can get it. Why not? He's rich and handsome and his name is respected by all. Besides, he has a palatial ancestral home to offer the current object of his affections.

That's right. Galahad wants a wife. A *perfect* wife, naturally, as he has carefully explained to his skeptical and chiding friends.

Galahad isn't the type of knight who rushes into things.

When he thinks he's found The Girl he has a whole checklist of qualities to measure her by. Is she exciting to the well-bred eye? Perfectly beautiful? Beautifully perfect? Charming in manner, flawless in taste, graceful in movement, conversationally delightful, of fine stock? Yes. Yes. Yes! And this one has a refined sensuality that steals his heart away. With much pomp and circumstance, Galahad and Cinderella marry, the absolutely *perfect* couple.

Only Cinderella doesn't think so. At night her knight is clumsy, and in the daytime dreary. She has her own checklist for the perfect man and Galahad just doesn't measure up. But she's a clever young lady and figures that *one* man can't possibly offer everything. So she gets herself several. One to talk with—the articulate, encyclopedia type; one to sleep with—an artist in the field of love; and one to be married to—that's Galahad, remember? Excellent family.

Galahad almost throws himself into the moat when he realizes what has happened to his perfect marriage. But suicide is so sensational! He'd divorce Cinderella, but that would be admitting failure before the world, and to himself. And besides, his friends would taunt and tease him forever and, of course, he couldn't bear losing face after all of his bragging. No, he decides. The only thing to do is to keep up a perfect front.

The Perfectionist's fear of ridicule creates an unbreakable bond between him and his wife. The secret humiliation he suffers through her activities is preferable to the public scorn of the divorce court. The Perfectionist knows that the world likes to see a man humbled, especially if he has pretended to be better than the philistines around him.

THE MAN WHO IS IN LOVE WITH LOVE

Naturally he is young and lovable, healthy, full of the zest of living. He is—for the time being—an incorrigible optimist.

There are bad things in life, he sagely admits, but it is childish to worry about them. Everything is curable or changeable. Of course he feels that people are wonderful. Everything is hunky-dory!

A charming imbecile, wouldn't you say? He hasn't the slightest premonition that life isn't all sunshine but can be as ugly as sin. Let me repeat: this character has stars in his eyes. He considers himself an unrecognized and smiling Hercules, cheerfully carrying the troubles of the world on his broad shoulders. He doesn't mind it a bit. As I see it, he is a strong character and his physical make-up and his background must correspond with his exuberant spirit. His actions naturally will grow out of his unbounded optimism which, of course, is proof-positive of his naiveté.

This man is a perfect foil for a farce comedy. He might fall in love with every attractive woman he meets and propose marriage to each, whether they be as young as he is or as old as his mother. Perhaps he will narrow the field to three, and ask each of them to be his wife. He decides the third one is the girl of his dreams, but how will he get rid of the other two?

Unfortunately, they both travel in the same social circle that he does. It is imperative that he get out of his difficulty as gracefully as possible without leaving a messy aftermath.

He tries to backtrack with the first. As he stammers, embarrassed and unintelligible, she interrupts with the news that she is in love with another man. She hopes he can appreciate her great problem. The young man is hurt and humiliated. But worst of all, he discovers that he never really loved anyone else—only her. His smarting ego assures him he will never be able to love anyone else! He threatens to die rather than give her up.

His eloquence and desperation convince the young girl that theirs is a great love, the like of which happens only in fairy tales. As they fall into each other's arms and swear eternal love, she promises to break off with the other man. After the great jubilation is over, the young man realizes he is now in a worse position than before.

How can he solve his problem? How can he retain his eternal optimism? Is everything as curable as he thought? His trouble is that he is physically and mentally young, unsophisticated, unspoiled. The story or play catches him as he is growing up. This, then, is not just an idea but a character maturing before our eyes.

An idea will never make a story, but a character will.

FATHERS AND SONS

I have to tell you a queer incident that happened between me and a young friend. He quite often complained of his malfunctioning liver. One day, as a joke, I told him he should sue his parents, not only for the suffering they had thoughtlessly passed on to him but for the endless doctor bills he was obliged to pay. He laughed at the joke, and then dropped the subject.

But the next time I saw him he told me that his doctor had advised an operation. I told him again, quite seriously, that he should sue his parents. I expanded my idea. Shouldn't someone set a precedent for punishment of parents who thoughtlessly bring innocent children into the world to suffer endless agonies all of their lives? It is against the law, I argued, to annoy, abuse, or hurt others. Why then should there not be a law against those who actually cripple their own offspring?

He looked at me, startled, and said, with a strange fire in his eyes, that he was going to write a novel on that theme. There is a law now that every couple who are going to marry have to take tests for venereal disease. Why not a law forbidding people to marry who might pass on other crippling sicknesses to their children?

I am sure this is a mad idea. But if you can visualize those who would accept such an idea and be willing to go through with it, you're going to have a hell of a good time making a story or play out of it. If it turns out to be as good as it is sensational, some writer—you? —will make a lot of money!

THE GRAY MAN

There's something peculiar about this man. He might have red hair, wear a navy-blue suit with a snow-white shirt and red necktie. Still you have the impression you are talking to a man who is all gray. You know without asking that whatever Bob Daniel does in the future will be tainted gray. You could swear he has never done a thing in his life which might be called colorful.

Bob Daniel is polite to everyone, not subservient, just a bit too correctly polite. If you should enter his home you could not fail to notice that even the walls match the furniture and the furniture matches his character. You get the impression you are in a comfortable but uninspiring apartment. Bob Daniel fits as perfectly here as a Yale key fits into a Yale lock.

There's only one problem. His wife Theresa doesn't fit into the pattern. She is a constantly moving element in this inert gray conformity—a nervous red spot in all this grayness. Her voice is sharp, full of vibrating, electrifying gall and hate. She loathes her husband, her home, her life. She married Bob because she feared becoming an old maid. The gray man was the only male in the whole world who could tolerate, let alone live with, her. By the same token, he knew she was the only woman who would tolerate his unexciting, phlegmatic nature.

At least once she cursed him to make him angry. But Bob Daniel was never angry. In the forty years of their marriage she failed to arouse him. Theresa often said, "One of these days you'll cut my throat, you murderer! Still water runs deep." She was actually frightened by his coolness, but Bob only smiled and let her holler. Anyone could see she was wrong. Bob Daniel would never hurt a fly. But then one day Theresa got hold of his prized Meerschaum pipes. (He was allowed to smoke only in the basement.) She broke them to pieces with an axe.

That evening Bob Daniel walked into the police station and told the attending officer, in his typically colorless way, that he had just murdered his wife. The officer at first considered it a joke—refused to believe it. But it was only too true!

But Bob Daniel remained gray even after he committed that horrible murder.

Is there really such a thing as a gray man? Of course not. The grayness was only a camouflage—just as exhibitionism is a camouflage—to hide the real, the frightened person behind it.

THE EXHIBITIONIST

She is a good-looking young woman about thirty—a platinum blonde who wears tight-fitting, low-cut dresses. Real whistle bait! You'd never dream she is married and has three children.

It's no secret. We all try to exhibit out greatest attribute. For Virginia Lee Matson, it is her feminine allurement. She is proud of what she has to show. Apparently, it is much in demand, judging from the remarks heard about her on the street. Her face is a masterpiece of craftsmanship—the perfect artwork on a soulless mannikin. But there's action elsewhere! Her bosom moves rhythmically, harmonizing with the undulation of her well-shaped buttocks.

Obviously, she's an exhibitionist. But this does not mean we know her. She may *look* like a call girl, but she is not. As I mentioned before, she is married and has three beautiful children. Why then does she dress and walk as she does, exhibiting herself to men, inspiring their lust and, at the same time, the hatred of her own sex?

If we answer this, we have a good story. Let me try to give you a skeleton sketch of her background.

She was married at sixteen. She hated John, her husband, even more than the hoodlum who caused her pregnancy and then disappeared. Actually, John was a good man—a bookkeeper. His only sin was marrying her on the rebound. He was the boy next door, who had loved Virginia since childhood. But she never gave him a thought. Nevertheless, when she found she was pregnant and her mother stopped her suicide attempt, it was John who came to the rescue. He took her away from a hopeless situation—gladly married her even though he knew she was pregnant.

But John's goodness did not influence Virginia. "You are the last man on earth I would have married," she'd tell him when in one of her frequent angry moods. She called him "Elderly"—his middle name which they both hated—to irritate him. "You act elderly to me," she whined. "I feel I'm in bed with an old man."

John was twenty-six at the time of their marriage. He was well-built, intelligent—even good-looking, though no one could convince Virginia of this fact. Any decent girl would have been happy to have him. But Virginia was neither decent nor rational. Deep down in her subconscious she hated him because he took possession of her when she had no choice. It was either death, disgrace, or John Elderly Matson. She tried death but ended up with John. She could never forgive him or herself for having married him under compulsion.

This is the superficial background of a young woman who is an exhibitionist.

There are other exhibitionists busily calling attention to themselves with their personalized idiosyncracies. Some of the most fascinating give sulking performances.

It works wonders. Try it yourself at a gay party. It's especially effective if you are a girl—and good-looking. Simply look morose, blank, bored, even disgusted with the revelers. Never a smile should cross your austere face. As sure as death someone will ask you—"Anything wrong?"

You'll answer, "Nothing." "Would you like a sandwich or something?" "No, thanks," you say. I am also sure that someone will surely volunteer to sit beside you. He'll probably say, "Boring, isn't it?" "Oh, I don't know," you say evasively. Your answer does not necessarily mean that you are antisocial. The man will try to hit upon a subject which might lead to an interesting discussion, If he fails, you might suggest a topic. If the man is bright, you'll have a wonderful time and, after a while, with a tolerant smile, you may suggest, "It's too noisy in here." If he lives nearby he will suggest, "Let's have a drink at my place. It is cozy and quiet there and we can talk." You might walk out triumphantly. You might even end up at his place if that is what you want, or somewhere else.

One thing is sure. Your sulking exhibition did a wonderful job. You've gotten a man. If he is not your type, you can try it again and again until the right man comes along. Sulking is a good trick! Sometimes it is even profitable.

There is no man, woman or child who would not try to be an exhibitionist if they could.

There is, however, an art to disguising oneself in order to project an attitude that presents something more noble than self-advertisement.

Under the disguise of—let's say—exhibitionism, might lurk a shy person. Exhibitionism is the product of frustration which later hardens into desperation. There might be thousands of different reasons why a person would become an exhibitionist, but, whatever the motivation, it is covering up the real individual behind the front. Strange to say, under the mask of a killer might hide a misunderstood coward who is ready to take revenge against mankind for his frustration.

Could a person be an exhibitionist without being aware of it? The next character, "The Crusader," will answer that question.

THE CRUSADER

He is the most gratifying man you have ever met. Good looking, very pleasant, very obliging, even self-sacrificing to anyone who has the good fortune to know him. No, he's not a big game hunter, nor a man who craves dangerous adventures.

He is a crusader. It is easy to recognize what he is. You need not talk to him for five minutes before he starts fingering the lapel of your jacket or, if you happen to be in shirt sleeves he will ask you casually, "How much did you pay for this thing?"

You will know instantly from his contemptuous tone that he thinks very little of your shirt or your suit. You name a price and whatever the figure, the great crusader will declare with much authority that you have been robbed.

That's it! He's the famous bargain-hunter. All of us like to get a bargain but he is passionate about this subject. He ferrets out a bargain wherever he hears of it. If there should be an article for a penny less than in the store nearest him, he'll pay more for traveling than what he saves. But he's almost religious about the matter. If you happen to be skeptical about his crusade, he'll threaten you with his philosophy on life in general, and on bargain-hunting in particular.

The immortality of the soul, the tremendous upheaval of the world transforming colonialism to self-governments, or the impending atomic world war are all bagatelles to the Great Crusader. Pinching pennies here or there is what counts for him. If you think he is a selfish man you are mistaken. In fact, he is willing to spend hours on a Saturday afternoon, dragging you to where you can buy whatever you want at a bargain price.

No doubt about it. He is not a character you can dismiss without a struggle. He offers his services gratis. What has made this man a passionate bargain-hunter? Poverty is not the only answer.

I happen to know a man who is a multi-millionaire and he is still pinching pennies. For a poverty-stricken person to save a penny is normal. But it's not normal for a rich man, despite his righteous indignation against cutthroats who are out to rob you. This bargain-hunter is a crusader. A penny saved actually means nothing to him. But the result is an exalted triumph, a superior achievement, a victory over the enemy. This bargain-hunter must feel superior to others who let themselves be hoodwinked.

(I have seen young children freely offer their dolls or toys to playmates, while others the same age grab what isn't theirs —hoarding, but never giving. Such symptoms of character traits are apparent in infancy. It must have something to do with inherited characteristics, which are discussed in the chapter on "X-Raying a Character.")

Suppose this bargain-hunter falls in love with a woman who is his opposite—a spendthrift. There is a definite challenge here and he feels he can change the pattern of her life. What a fallacy!

Nevertheless, he truly believes he can make a convert and prove that miracles are possible.

Then the fun begins! Before marriage, she hastens to agree with the bargain-hunter's logic. She is in her late thirties and eager to wed. He is, as I mentioned before, a pleasant indi-

vidual with a lucrative position. She hastily takes his out-
stretched hand and becomes filled with the best intentions of
becoming a good wife and a brand new personality. The resolutions last a year or more, perhaps, but slowly the imper-
ceptible change comes into their lives. The battle-royal begins, which might culminate in divorce with a heartbreaking
defeat for both.

THE HAPPY MAN

It is easy to recognize a happy man. He's cheerful and full
of delightful stories. He offers good advice to everyone.
Above all, he is a lifelong advocate of optimism. He is not
afraid of anything on earth—except sorrow. And he is as
afraid of that as the day is of the night. No doubt he has a
woman devoted to him. He has no financial worries and it is
heartwarming to hear him say to everyone, "Money isn't
everything." (You can bet your last farthing that a man who
makes such a remark has no financial worries!)

Naturally, the happy man is as healthy as an ox. His stride
is springy. He breathes deeply and he can boast of a ready
smile on a pink, rounded face.

He declares loudly his unquestioning belief in Norman
Vincent Peal's *Positive Thinking*. He wouldn't recognize evil
even if it should punch him in the nose. He's fashioned after
that famous Queen who is said to have told the howling,
hungry mob, "If they have no bread, let them eat cake."
Furthermore, this happy man's digestion is superb. (Without
that, neither money nor positive thinking could make him
happy.)

I'm aware that for a starving writer, a happy man is neither
the best nor the most lucrative theme. Most readers do not
know that happy people are the worst subjects to write about.
They are dull because nothing exciting happens around
them. Writers thrive on unhappiness and crime. The well-

known slogan that crime doesn't pay is true for general consumption, but not for writers.

Still, there is no man who can be happy twenty-four hours a day. Everybody is made of the same ninety-six elements. Consequently, we all share some kind of anxieties. Fears, little ids, superegos all play havoc at times with our subconscious. I have no doubt that our man must wonder how long this happy state of mind will last. What if he should develop cancer? Then all the money in the world won't help him feel complacent again. What if the man's beloved wife isn't as happy with him as he is with her? His confidence and stability would be destroyed if she disappeared with another man.

There are developments at every turn which could ruin his happiness. His ideal wife, a source of comfort in the past, might stay with him for the rest of his life. But what happens if she slowly becomes ossified by the humdrum sameness, a coma dulling her mind?

It is useless to say that the state of being static is non-existent. One thing changes into another. The future becomes the present. Our present will be the past. It is inevitable that after day comes night. Let the happy man walk with an aura of optimism about him. There is still a story in him for a lucky writer who can discover the lurking unhappiness in the happy man.

THE INDISPENSABLE MAN

He is a good man. The fact is—he is so good that he would love to help the whole world. But since he's smart enough to know he can't help everybody, he's settled down to help only those around him. He is sensitive to the breaking point. He cries easily. Please don't tell him any hard-luck stories because he won't be able to eat or sleep afterward.

Strangly enough, his wife left him after fifteen years of marriage, claiming mental cruelty. This man, who could sympathize with his worst enemy, could never feel sympathetic toward his own wife. When she divorced him he was naturally outraged by her unreasonable demands for alimony.

Let's have a closer look at this humanitarian, Renard Bara, before we pass judgment on him. His heart could break just caring for others.

He was a real estate operator, a multi-millionaire. He had the Midas touch. Whaetver he did turned into hard cash, bonds, stocks, gold. He had tremendous holdings, although he gave lavishly to charity. If there was an emergency in Asia, Africa, or anywhere in the world, Renard Bara was there to help.

This fine human being had no children of his own. After the tragedy of his divorce, he refused the idea of marriage. A nephew, his sister's son Eric, was his favorite. He adopted him when he was only five years old. He schooled him and sent him to college. In fact, he looked after him as if he were his own legitimate son.

And what about his sister? What kind of woman would give her son for adoption even to a rich brother? I really hate to drag the sister into this story, but logic is organized reason. I must, against my better judgment, say a few words about this affair.

Renard Bara did not talk to his own sister for God knows how many years. She was ten years older than he—a notorious gossip who made trouble for everyone. Her one-time friends grew to hate and despise her. In return she became a relentless avenger, digging up dirt about everyone and trumpeting it all over town. She hated Renard more than all of her enemies combined. The reason? While Renard was young, she had advised him about a profession—what to do with his life if he wished to be rich. Renard listened dutifully, but went along with his own ideas. He succeeded fabulously. Every step brought him more riches and more hatred from his sister.

Renard's great success was a thorn in her side, for she knew her suggestions would have led him to failure and penury. When her husband died, she was left with four children, sustained by public home relief. That's when Renard asked to adopt five-year-old Eric. She consented only if he, in return, would give her $75 a week for the rest of her life. Renard consented with the understanding that as long as she lived, she would never call him nor come near his home. To break the promise meant a discontinuance of his payments.

I must make at least one statement about this maddeningly stupid arrangement. The sister could have asked for $200, $300, or even $500 a week. She would have received it without a word. But this miserable woman was so small, not only in stature but also in heart and imagination that she thought $75 a large sum of money, although Renard was a very rich man.

Eric had everything money could buy. His adoptive father had given him all a young man could wish for. And yet when he finished college, Renard of the sympathetic heart received the greatest shock of his life. Eric not only refused to work with his father but asked to move out of his house to start a new life of his own.

Arguments, pro and con, lasted for weeks. There was a feeling of bitterness between them, but Eric was adamant to the end.

Then a strange transformation started in the sympathetic heart of Renard. He set out to prove, with the determination of a crusader, that Eric would never amount to anything without his help. The change in Renard from kindness to cruelty was slow and subtle at first. But facing the young man's obdurate struggle for independence aroused in him an unreasoning vindictiveness to destroy him rather than forsake his unshakeable belief that without him he could never be a success.

Under the façade of kindness, cruelty hardened into frightening ferocity. Renard's ego was slighted, and now he was ready to destroy the one he loved more than his own life.

THE EGOCENTRIC MAN

The first words that Steve Berna uttered as he flung open my office door were, "The dirty little bitch!" He hurried in, his handsome face an angry red, and stopped before my desk. He looked at me with glazed eyes as if he were going to throw some wild, irresponsible words into my face. But after a moment's hesitation he slumped lifelessly into a chair. Spoken words had lost all meaning in his hopelessness. His head dropped into his hands, and then this big man started to sob unashamedly.

He was sixty years old, but he looked much younger. He had the body of a well-trained wrestler. But instead of a dehumanized face, he looked and acted as if he were the president of some sort of respectable institution.

From the few mumbled words I heard, I began to realize what must have happened to him. The young woman he had picked up in the slums five years before had walked out on him. When they met she was a slender eighteen with the face of a blue-eyed angel. He bought expensive dresses for her, furnished a cozy little apartment in the West 70's, and sent her to school. He took her to the theatre and lectures and, in short, made a respectable little lady out of her.

He was a real estate operator. His wife, a rich widow, was not pretty, and her obnoxious nagging did not help to keep his marital fire burning. Steve was a pleasant fellow. His love for Gloria (her original name was Marlie) deepened with the years. He gave her mink coats, diamonds, and beautiful clothes. Any day he did not see her was a lost day.

Steve threw a crumpled piece of paper on my desk, mumbling like a man who had lost his mental faculties. There were just a couple of lines on the paper:

"This is goodby for good, lover boy. Sorry. I'm going to get married. Gloria."

"The dirty little bitch! I've given her everything."

His helplessness was infuriating. Who the devil did he think he was? A schoolboy of sixteen? He insisted time and again that he had given her everything. But I knew the jewelry, furs, and fineries were not acts of kindness. Not even of love. They were all bare-faced bribes to chain her to him for his pleasure. Should I tell him? Will he understand that we never never do anything for anyone?

Was this the time to explain to a distraught man that all the kindnesses, all the good deeds we perform, first of all must give us pleasure and importance? Would he understand that even love in its purest form, or the noble filial death-defying attachment, is nothing more than an act for our satisfaction, for our safety, and for our happiness?

I decided not to discuss these points just then. He understood by my pat on his shoulder that I was sympathizing with his great sorrow. As he squeezed my hand in return he asked with a barely recognizable voice: "What shall I do?"

"Apparently she thought her clandestine affair with you was not making her happy," I answered. "She did not leave you for another man, Steve. She left you for marriage—a home and perhaps children."

I knew he would not buy this explanation, but I was sure that he would feel better knowing that Gloria had left him for the only thing he could not give her—marriage. A divorce, in Steve's case, would have started a disaster for him.

With the above story, I wished to demonstrate that the success or failure of any type of writing depends on the real

misguided motivations of characters and the correct understanding by writers of the characters they intend to expose.

Beckett's *Waiting for Godot* was a simple statement, as far
as I am concerned. The play affirms that no one, including
God, will help any of us. We must get along alone. Or, "God
helps those who help themselves."

Let a play be presented in the most outlandish and distorted manner, still the author must have something vital in
his mind in order to write his opus. Not all plays come
through, of course, as the author intended.

Endgame, also by Beckett, where Man—the last ossified
specimen—remains one desolate burned-out Globe, mystified
people no end. To me, it was full of desperate meaning. "Get
up, Man," the author cried, "and try to live! Settle the pitiful
differences between you. Live while living is good and possible."

Motivation is the key to understanding. Even a murderer
has his own good reasons to fortify himself for the ordeal
ahead. Motivation, justification, rationalization, vilification,
and even distortion are the basis of human conflict.

Steve Berna, the man who lost his mistress, was staggered
when I told him his generosity was actually not directed to
Gloria but to himself. Of course he wouldn't accept my interpretation of his conduct. He was absolutely sure that
everything he did was right. She willingly came to him, and
he was generous. It was the same old thing. He tried to hammer into my head that the girl was an ingrate, a gold-digger,
an unreliable no-good hussy who would come to no good
end.

No one likes to see himself in an unfavorable light. In his
bitterness he turned against his wife. If she had been young
and beautiful all this would not have happened, he reasoned.
But she was not young and she certainly was not beautiful.
However, she was rich. Now he conveniently forgot that
without her he would never have had the opportunity to be

the top man in any organization. He was looking for trouble. He was bickering and fighting with his wife. And at the end of one maddening quarrel he threatened to get a divorce! His wife quite calmly accepted the challenge. She knew too well he would be left penniless in the case of a divorce, so once more he was forced to his knees to sample the bitter taste of humiliation. Reluctantly, he was ready to explain, to apologize, to rationalize, and vilify innocent people who had supposedly caused him to turn against his own beloved wife!

She accepted the face-saving solution. But not Steve. His ego was too badly bruised. He made up his mind to find Gloria. He did find her and boldly, angrily, self-righteously stepped into her life and demanded that she become his mistress again. She was married and happy. Frightened, she begged him to leave her alone and not to break up her marriage. He did not leave her alone. In his blindness he insisted. Her husband gave him the beating of his life. Then came scandal—his picture in all the tabloids. His wife, who had known all along of his indiscretions, at last divorced him!

There are many possible ways to end this story. Gloria might have been thrown out by her husband, found Steve and demanded protection. But the difference between a wife and a mistress is so wide that it is insurmountable. What then?

I don't care what type of character one writes about if he has his own crystalized ideas, philosophy about tradition, about books, politics, marriage, science and about almost everything. Whether I agree with him or not, he expresses himself and I shall recognize what he really is.

The Girl of Tomorrow

Here is an idea with a built-in character.

A young lady stands in the middle of the room, talking to an admiring male audience.

"I might as well tell you that our moral outlook is outmoded, antiquated, almost barbaric. Women are afraid to talk about our double standard. What cowardice! Women should have the moral courage to revolt and say openly that the male approach to sex is the most healthy impulse to follow. They eliminated their feelings of guilt. They acted guiltlessly, as men who are not afraid to say they are hungry and would love to eat something exotic. It should be the same when the hunger is for sex."

I can go on. There is the man who is absolutely sure the earth is flat. The person who believes that all conflict between men, and men and nations, could be eliminated if people would decide to go stark naked. In short—the salvation of mankind is nudity!

They say the hog dreams of corn. Lots of corn. A man with a ventilated head dreams of a woman who salaams whenever her incomparable husband comes home from work. He wants her to fall flat on her face so her Ruler can step on her like a doormat!

Of course, an author must know *why* this character needs such a subservient woman. Why does he think that marriage is what he needs instead of a well-functioning liver, or a couch in the office of a psychoanalyst?

If you write about a self-centered man, let him not be just a little self-centered. He might be a physicist, or a moron, or a professor of classical literature—still he can exhibit a virulent, full-fledged stupidity about women.

Q. Where do writers get their ideas?

A. From characters, of course.

Q. But did you find the answer to your problem—activating your characters to create conflict?

A. I did. It seems all these people act under a terrific compulsion. I am sure the stingy character went through hell to remain faithful to his conviction—fear of tomorrow. He committed one mistake: he dared to fall in

love and marry. The rest of the story is the natural outgrowth of his miscalculation.

It is the same tragedy with the perfectionist. He
wants a perfect mate but his mistake is that he is far
from being perfect. Sorrow and life-long humiliation
follow.

After I finished reading *The Man Who Is in Love
with Love* I understood at last what was wrong with
me. All these characters have an inborn or acquired
compulsive drive to escape some kind of injury. With
the first wrong step they find themselves in trouble,
sinking in quicksand. While they struggle to save their
very lives, they find new and worse handicaps before
them. It is not up to them any more whether they want
to fight or not. They must—if they wish to survive.

Q. Very good. Tell me. Was there a compulsive drive in
the man who was in love with love?

A. Yes. His exuberant optimism, his lack of foresight and
experience. He not only made love, but an irresistible
and foolish impulse drove him to propose marriage to
everyone he made love to. It seems he has no control
over his impulses. But he is in good company. Macbeth,
the ruthlessly ambitious general, had a compulsive
desire to become king. Hamlet had a compulsive drive
for revenge. Tartuffe had a compulsive lust for Orgon's
wife. The junk dealer in *Born Yesterday* was com-
pelled to corner the market whatever the cost. Jesus's
compulsive drive against hypocrisy and his fight for the
underprivileged drove him to Golgotha. Michelan-
gelo's childhood compulsion to sculpt made him at last
immortal.

I realize now that if I want my protagonist to move I
must create a character who acts compulsively, mov-

ing blindly and inevitably toward his destiny, whether it leads to heaven or hell.

Q. I am glad you have finally found the answer. Now go ahead and write. Will you?

A. You just try to stop me!

II

Any idiosyncracy, habit, phobia, or hypersensitivity in a character leads a writer to an important source of material.

Here is a brief sketch of a character with an unusual idiosyncracy.

For as long as she could remember, Charlotte had been "madly in love with cats." About a year before she met Bill, her future husband, she bought the most beautiful, the sweetest, Siamese cat in existence. It was pedigreed, too, she boasted. Aware of her passion for cats, Charlotte knew this tremendous emotional relationship with a dumb animal might lead her to a bad end.

Needless to say, Bill, who married her for love, was appalled by her unnatural devotion to Esteg, as she chose to call her precious Siamese cat.

She could never bear to leave him alone in the house. Wherever she went, the cat was her constant companion. Even on her honeymoon, Esteg watched the intimate proceedings between the lovers until Bill, infuriated, got hold of the animal by the scruff of his neck, threw him into the bathroom and banged the door shut.

Charlotte screamed and ran to free her pet, but Bill sternly warned that if she opened the door their marriage would come to an end—right then and there. She stopped, of course, but their relationship from that moment on became strained.

Charlotte knew that her behavior was unnatural. She tried her very best to make Bill look on Esteg as a friend rather than an enemy. He tried to understand, but the cat was inconsolable. It was silent warfare between Esteg and Bill.

One single human trait could be the foundation for a gripping story. The first question the author must answer is: Why is Charlotte so mad about Siamese cats? Why do cats in general play such an important part in her life? If the writer wishes to write an absorbing tale he must let us know how far Charlotte is willing to go to protect her cat from her husband.

Voltaire's *Candide* is a bitter satire on the concept that "all is for the best in this best of all possible worlds." Candide finds a woman who loves him dearly. Right after that, his father-in-law kicks him out of his estate. War breaks out. Candide is forced into the army. His wife is raped, becomes the mistress of the Inquisitor, and is mutilated by pirates. He survives illness, shipwreck, shooting, and all manner of disasters one after the other, until he becomes very old and ill. But this good, simple-minded man never loses his optimism.

There is no such phenomenon in nature as a 100-percent optimist, so Candide stands before us as an impossible specimen. But Voltaire knew what he was doing. By exaggeration, he directs the reader's attention toward his own shortcomings. When Candide's optimism is idiotic, it makes the reader ashamed of himself.

In *Hamlet,* the prince's goal is to avenge the murder of his beloved father. We know that his father's ghost has told him of the crime, but Hamlet's insistence on finding out for himself what actually happened holds us spellbound.

The Silver Cord by Sidney Howard is also a case in point. The mother's iron determination to keep her sons for herself is the core of the play.

Suppose you have one crystalized character with a maniacal urge to commit a crime or sacrifice himself for a noble cause.

Such a character would make you write a fine story or play about him. You work on it (who knows how long), and after a heroic struggle, it is finished. You feel you are justified in expecting praise for your hard labor—but for some mysterious reason the characters never come to life.

What could have happened? I will tell you what actually happened. You did not know your character as an author should.

Here is an interesting story to contemplate.

You, the writer, find yourself in a singularly dangerous situation. Let me emphasize: *you,* and not the character you are writing about, find yourself in a small boat with your beautiful, beloved wife, your sweet little daughter, and your mother, the greatest mother who ever lived. The small boat is sinking. Rowing becomes impossible and none of you can swim.

You hope that a plane may have sighted you and gone for a helicopter to save you, but now your business is to manage to stay afloat.

The boat, under the combined weight, continues to sink. One of you must sacrifice his life to save the others. Who will be the first? Your wife? Your daughter? Or your mother? Not you, because without you they would perish in minutes.

If you think this is a tragic situation, then you don't know what a really tragic situation is. One of you, by her own choice, sacrifices herself for the rest of the family. Of course it is your mother. She willingly gives her life for the family.

Only the three of you remain, your wife, your daughter and you. The boat is sinking deeper. Another must go. Who do you think it will be? Your wife hysterically argues that her daughter should stay alive. Suddenly she slips into the water —to save not you, but her child.

You are alone with the last of your family. You and your daughter. This is the most critical time of the desperate situation. Will you sacrifice your life that your child may live?

Don't be hasty. Think it over. If you go, the child probably will not survive without your help.

You, the author, must give the answer to this dilemma. It is your story. It is your life and no one else's. You see, every character must be you and yet, when you let your mother and your wife drift under the water, no matter how heartbreaking it was, it still was not you. But now the life-and-death struggle is between you and your daughter. Which will be the one? Will you let your daughter die to prolong your life for a short while or will you try to go down with her? If you can imagine that, your answer will concern your life and not that of a fictional character; your description of the death struggle will be so real, so devastating that you etch an indelible picture on the reader's mind that will endure for years to come.

Q. All this is very well, but a story or a play might have another type of story to tell than that of an opinionated man trying to force his will on his opponents.

A. Tell me one.

Q. I can't think of one at this moment, but there must be other approaches.

A. Let's imagine there is a nice quiet town somewhere in the world. People there have known each other since childhood.

Their ancestors lived there side by side for centuries. They have their customs, religion, and nothing out of the ordinary ever happens to them. Conformity blooms there unchallenged. These people act and think alike; even their tastes in food, in color, in morals, run in the same direction. Like bees, they are almost indistinguishable from one another.

The question is, what can happen with such peaceful, loving people?

I will tell you what can happen. Bring in one single

individual who has different ideas, morals, religion, and you will see ferocious conflict.

Q. How about love?

A. What kind of love?

Q. I mean love. Period.

A. There are many kinds of love. Frustrated love, for one. Possessive love for another. This is the same approach I was discussing before. Any kind of love, if it is strongly felt, will be as good as the force of hate or vengeance could be.

Q. How about love of fishing?

A. If it is as strong as 100 percent, it can break up a marriage, dissolve a partnership, or even lead to murder. The point I am trying to make is that whatever a writer wants to say must be direct and compulsive in the character. Shyness can be as compulsive as anything under the sun. A wishy-washy emotion or a vacillating directive will lead your manuscript to where it belongs —the wastebasket!

Let's consider the role hypersensitivity plays in character.

Humiliate, hurt, or just contradict a supersensitive man only once and he'll build a case against you which will not only endure but will grow in proportion and in coloration the rest of his natural life.

People are strange and complicated. I am sorry to say that many years ago one outburst on my part destroyed the most beautiful friendship I ever had.

I had a beautiful dog of mixed breed, half collie and half shepherd, called Chang. He not only acknowledged me as his master but elevated me to the exalted position of being his personal god. Every evening after dinner Chang and I used to sit in a Morris chair reading our paper. This was a nightly ritual.

Then one evening something happened that completely upset our idyllic routine. I had had the kind of day when everything I did went wrong. Naturally, my evening was even worse, for I had time to reflect upon all the stupidities I had committed during the day.

I was in an explosive temper and started to read my paper —tried to read it would be more accurate—without having eaten my dinner first. As usual Chang was prompt, but the moment he put his intelligent head on my knee, announcing "I am here," I said sternly, "Listen here, Chang, let me alone tonight. I'm in a bad mood. Understand?"

There was nothing strange in talking to him as if he were human; we always had, and he always seemed to understand. But not tonight. Tonight he elected to play dumb. He stood looking up at me with the innocence of an infant. Gently but determinedly I lifted his head from my knee and said once more, "Not tonight. Go away."

He retreated a few steps, sat on his haunches and waited. I thought I had gotten rid of him. I made another futile attempt to read, trying hard to forget the whole miserable day. Suddenly I realized that Chang was halfway up on my lap. I was irritated beyond control, and with a curse I pushed him to the floor. He fell with a dull thud.

I felt instant remorse. "Please Chang, I'm sorry, awfully sorry, but can't you see I'm sick and tired tonight? Why can't you let me alone?"

He just sat there and looked at me and it seemed as if he had understood, because his bushy tail wagged once. It meant "All right. Let's forget it."

I started to read again, but Chang concluded that since I had apologized and he had nobly forgiven me, he could take his customary place on my lap.

But the moment he came near I felt as if an electric current had touched me, and, almost jumping out of my chair, I

shouted: "Damn you, get the hell out of here. . . ! Get out!"
Even as I said it I was sorry. His tail between his legs, Chang
retreated, frightened and shaking.

"See what you've done?" I told him, pleadingly. "Why
can't you let me alone for one single evening?"

He understood the tone of my voice. It sounded concilia-
tory and he was happy once more. He just couldn't believe
that I, his god, could suddenly be so unfair as to punish him
for doing something he had always done with my full approval. He started to approach me with his tail wagging. I
saw with dismay that he had misunderstood me again.

Wanting to be on the safe side, I said to him harshly, "No,
no, no! Do you understand? No! Go away!"

He stood stock still, his tail at half mast, looking at me
pitifully. Now he saw that I meant what I said. I took up my
paper with great determination and started to read. A moment or two later I looked up stealthily to see if he were
going to annoy me again. With great relief I saw that he was
going away at last.

If I had known what was coming, I would gladly have
apologized to him then and there, but I didn't and was glad
that at last I had made him understand that I wanted to be
left alone. He should learn a little discipline, I said to myself
with a righteous feeling, and with that I lost myself in my
paper.

The next day things righted themselves, as they usually do,
and I was in a much better mood. After dinner I sat in my
chair reading, when a feeling of uneasiness stole over me.
Something wasn't right. Why, of course, Chang was missing.
He wasn't sitting on my lap as he did every evening.

I called to him cheerfully, "Chang! Where are you, old
boy?"

He came charging in from the kitchen to see why I had
called him.

"Come here, boy, come on up. Let's read our paper."

He wagged his tail once but didn't move.

"Don't you want to come to me, old fellow?"

He stood there all attention, ready to obey any order—except that one. It was the first time he had ever been reluctant to do something I wished him to do. I felt a slight foreboding. I knew I had been brusque with him the night before, but for heaven's sake, I thought, life is not exactly milk and honey.

I started to pat my knee to show him in dumb language what I wanted, which was an insult as he was the most intelligent animal I had ever known. But now he refused to budge. His large brown eyes were focused on me, almost begging me to order him to do something else, anything, only not that humiliating experience of last night, please!

Wanting to re-establish our old comradeship, and seeing that no coaxing could make him change his mind, I decided to play a trick on his great, almost inordinate love for sweets. I took a big piece of sugar-coated cake from the icebox. Chang was at my heels as I walked back to the living room.

I sat down and he came slowly, very slowly, toward me. I smiled and thought, how easy it is! Just then, one step from me, he stopped and looked at me with great expectation.

"Come, come now, old boy. It's for you—this nice piece of cake." I showed it to him temptingly. He refused to be corrupted. I tried to coax him but I couldn't induce him to come into my lap. I was annoyed at last and said, "Whether you like it or not, old pal, you're going to sit in my lap as usual," and I got hold of his collar, pulled him toward me and lifted him up.

He stayed put, but I felt every muscle in his body tense. I told him to relax, that he didn't have to be afraid of me, and if he were afraid it was unfair because I had never hurt him before. My voice was reassuring, and I stroked his head. It seemed as if he understood me and I thought he would calm down, but he didn't. The moment he felt my grip loosen he jumped down.

This performance was repeated over and over again. From that day on, it was useless for me to try to make friends with him, although I tried very hard. I tried for weeks, without success. He never, until the day he died years later, forgave me for that one fateful evening.

And he was only a dog.

Oh merciful God! How sensitive a thinking human being can be, if even a dog acts like a human.

Is there a human being who has no desire to be important? Such a man never lived. Even a corpse in his majestic silence is full of frozen dignity. In the presence of such unbending respectability all flippancy is a sacrilege.

10

Introduction to Motivation

Motivation, reduced to its simplest definition, means *why*.

Motivation is that which prompts a person, or a character, to act in a certain way. Every action has a reason. Indeed, nothing ever happens on earth without motivation.

As a writer, you must constantly ask yourself *why* a person or a character acts as he does. You must determine the motivation.

How is this possible?

First, let's consider this.

All living characters have a certain universality about them. Human beings, let them be Greek, Roman, German, or American, are basically the same. Only the veneer—their customs, ethics, or social conformity—makes them *appear* different from each other. Their basic emotions and drives, such as hunger, fear, love, hate, devotion—are universal. Individuals feel them in different degrees of intensity. Emotions create motivation. A good place to begin the study of motivation would seem to be with ordinary people.

But who is ordinary?

The obvious answer is, a person who looks and acts the way

the majority do. If he is too handsome or too tall or too short, too fat, or too thin, he is not ordinary. The ordinary person is one who can lose himself in a crowd without attracting any special attention or interest. You look at ordinary people on the street and promptly forget their faces as though you had never seen them.

But actually, even the ones who can lose themselves in a crowd aren't ordinary. On the contrary, they are probably hypersensitive about their nondescript appearance. And to be hypersensitive isn't in the least ordinary. They probably curse their fate for their sameness, just as a man whose eyes are too close together curses that physical affliction. These nondescript persons may develop a fearful inferiority complex when they observe that others almost look through them. At all costs, they want to be noticed—by someone, somewhere, sometime.

How can they attract attention? Plain or drab-looking people accomplish this by their ingenuity, cleverness, eagerness to please, or their generosity. Great men and great women have come from their ranks.

Why should this be so?

Frustration and disappointment more often than not are the incentives to achieve something great. On the other hand, those who are very good-looking sit back complacently, amused, feeling quite secure in their appearance.

Then perhaps these good-looking people are really the normal ones.

No. If this were entirely true, then they would always remain deficient in those attributes which can make an average-looking person great.

It is obviously foolish to think that all attractive persons necessarily lack the qualities to be outstanding in some higher endeavor. They, too, have all the qualities that make others outstanding, but since they achieve acclaim, praise, even adulation, without special effort, their ability to achieve something worthwhile in the mental sphere may go unused. On the other hand, if an extraordinarily good-looking person is a thinking human being, he may believe that he has achieved certain prominence or attention only because of his attractiveness and not by any special effort on his part.

Consequently, these good-looking people can also develop devastating inferiority complexes. They may wish to live down their good looks and prove to the world that although they happen to be attractive, they still can be as intelligent and resourceful as others who are outstanding in their field.

Almost all those who draw attention in a crowd and also those who are rarely noticed want to live down something they consider undesirable for their complete well-being.

It seems reasonable, therefore, to draw the conclusion that there are no "ordinary" people.

Motivation moves silently behind all the personal turmoil that exists. Motivation is the culprit responsible for all that has happened and will happen.

As a writer, if you are introspective (and I trust you are), motivation is usually obvious in yourself. But frequently it is exceedingly difficult to detect in others. Because of this, the lack of it is one of the main reasons why plays, stories and novels fail.

Every character must have a past, a present, and a future. And in terms of these three dimensions, each one must talk, move, act, and grow. Characters who represent only the present, without any past and future, are straw men. Remember this. The *Present* is the child of *Yesterday* and the father of *Tomorrow*. In constructing believable characters, these three are indivisible elements.

All writers must gain a working understanding of these elements if they wish to succeed in their chosen field by design rather than by accident.

It is true that many one-shot successes are achieved by writers who do not consciously know *why* their characters behaved as they did. The reason is simply that the writer happened to stumble upon people he knew intimately. This close proximity to his characters supplied all the complicated mechanism that he needed for his writing. He knew them and knew the *motivations* that made them do what they did.

But these are the writers whose second, third, and fourth novels, plays, and stories never fulfill the promise offered by their first and single success.

If it were possible, and it is, to analyze and finally split the atom, I assure you that it is possible to chart the course of a good piece of literature or theatre before it is written.

Good writing is impossible without sound motivation.

All types of motivation, conflict, rationalization, exaggeration, boasting, lying are nothing but instruments for man to protect his hard-earned importance. For his hallowed ego, he builds bomb-proof shelters in case mankind shall die in a terrible holocaust. Whether he perishes or not, he will insist on an inscription on his tomb in giant proud letters—"Don't Disturb, I'm Still Important."

ENVIRONMENT

The sources of all motivations are the *physical make-up* of a person and his *environment*. His sensitivity or his brutality, his attitude toward himself and toward the world is shaped by the above-mentioned two sources.

Let me test this to see if it is true.

Some time ago I read a newspaper account of how Paul, an eleven-year-old shoeshine boy, innocently caused a death. It is a pitiful story.

Paul's father had been killed in an accident. His widow was left with three children and was without funds. Paul decided that shining shoes would bring in more money than running errands or delivering newspapers, so he built a wooden box and selected a busy corner not far from his home. He thought he was ready for business. He was ready, all right, but the fellow whose corner he had innocently taken had different and violent ideas.

When he arrived and saw a stranger in his usual place he attacked without asking questions or giving Paul a chance to explain. Paul resisted at first, but finding the other fellow too strong for him, broke away and ran. In the ensuing chase the other boy was run over and killed instantly by a truck.

This was the story I read. What follows is the result of my imagination.

The investigation into the death of Robert Remeto, age thirteen, took almost three weeks, but Paul was cleared of guilt. It was established beyond the shadow of a doubt that Robert had been crushed to death by a truck as he was chasing Paul.

Not long afterward, Paul appeared once more at the same subway station with his shoeshine box. The best place was just beside the candy store, a strategic position for catching the eye of a prospective customer. This had been Robert's envied spot, and after his death the next in line, Chico Marossa, a dark, lanky boy, took it over as his rightful legacy. He was tough, and the others readily accepted him as the arbiter in all their disputes. On the morning when Paul reappeared on the scene, he took his position before the candy store, naively assuming that with Robert dead, the place was open. He put his shoeshine box on the sidewalk and stood behind it, leaning against the red brick wall, ready for business.

He had come back to the same place instead of going elsewhere because, he told himself, he already knew a few of the boys in the neighborhood. The real motivation was that he knew the neighborhood better than any other. If worst came to worst, he could escape pursuers more easily on familiar terrain.

As the day wore on, the other boys who lived nearby looked at him with amazement and moved on without saying a word to him. This kid had caused the death of Robert Remero, the toughest guy around, and now he had come back for more. The boys' eyes held fear and respect, both powerful deterrents from being chummy with him. He is dangerous, they thought, and left him alone.

Paul watched the boys' guarded faces and knew there would be trouble again. He started to shiver inside. He felt as though millions of ants were crawling all over his body.

"Shine, Mister?" he cried, and didn't recognize his own voice. It was husky and throaty. "Shine? Shine, Mister?" No one was passing just then, but he hollered anyway. It showed courage. It said to the boys, "I'm here to stay! What're you gonna do about it?"

He remembered his mother's tearful eyes when he had left in the morning, begging him to take care of himself. He had promised and hurried away, afraid he might burst out crying. He felt like crying right now. He wanted to bury his head in her ample bosom, as he had done many times before. She loved him, and in sheer tenderness she used to squeeze him to herself. Paul was so happy at such moments that he wanted that feeling to stay with him the rest of his life.

Whenever he thought of this strange emotion toward his mother he was ashamed, but there was something brave in this feeling. He was challenging these boys right now because of it. A quiet voice within him said, "You could go somewhere else," but he knew that to obey it would be cowardly. It would mean betraying the trust of his mother.

"Shine? Shine, Mister?" As he looked up, he saw Chico Marossa, the roughneck, the boy whose place he had unknowingly usurped, standing before him. The boy's dark face be-

INTRODUCTION TO MOTIVATION

came darker as he looked at Paul. Paul gasped as he missed a heartbeat, and in that breathless moment he decided he would not run away even if he must die. He cried his defiance once more: "Shine, Mister?" Then he looked deliberately at Chico and said, "Do you want somethin'?"

Chico felt like smashing Paul's nose but he had been present at the funeral of Robert, his best friend. He had seen the peace of eternity on the yellow face. And now, as he looked at Paul, he recalled sickeningly that this skinny slob was the cause of his friend's death. Chico shivered as terror started to rattle his legs. A nameless fear gripped him and, without answering, he walked away with his shoeshine box.

I have always wanted to see how "environment" influences people, molding them into new shapes. It is the undisputed, ruthless, uncompromising Caesar of man. I've always wanted to know whether man submits or fights against the tyranny. What chance has he to escape from its bondage? What weapons can he use against this paralyzing "influence of environment"?

I think I know Paul quite well. I'll try to build a background for him. I know he defied a cruel beating because of his love for his stepmother. She gave him what he had never had before—his role of savior of her other children, his self-respect, his awakening of manhood, the need for making money, the fascination of seeing the world, the always exciting, new, and sometimes grotesque panorama of experiences he calls fun, and finally, greater security.

Right now, Paul is a nice boy, He is brave at the moment because cowardice would bring hunger, shame, and loss of the adoration of his brothers and sisters and the tenderness of his stepmother.

He is really frightened, but the boys on the street are afraid of him. Robert, the tough guy who wanted to kill him a few weeks ago, now by his death is protecting him from further attack. The memory of this untimely death is a monument to Paul's invincibility. The conception of death is actually vague to these boys. It doesn't mean dissolution, dust to dust, as far as they are concerned. They know the boy is dead and buried, but the important thing is that Paul made it impossible for him to come back to his usual haunts. Because of him, Robert is in the cemetery, and the boys remember how they hate to go near a cemetery, even in the daytime.

There stands Paul, with the mysterious and invisible "influence of environment" all around him. Although it can't be seen, it is working on him constantly. He is standing there, up to his neck in environment. Environment does not consist only of people. It is also houses, the streets he lives and walks on. Even gasoline fumes are part of it.

Environment is everywhere. It is the gray sky, and it is a stuffy apartment on the fifth floor of a tenement. The crying babies, the cursing mothers, the drunken fathers also belong, and perhaps they build a horror against squalling babies with eternally dirty, runny noses. I must remember the food Paul eats, his father, and his real mother, the grocery-store flat where he was conceived and then born, everything living and dead, all the noises he ever heard, all the smells he ever smelled, the lights and shadows, and the bedbugs in the beds, for all these are environment. Even the dreams that he dreamed, the thoughts he thought, are a part of the whole and of him.

So there stands Paul, with his shoeshine box, and he would never believe it if someone were to tell him that he too is a part of environment for others. But he is, and slowly he realizes that the boys are genuinely afraid of him. This realization takes time, of course. At last Paul lets go of fear and gradually starts to expand. His face loses its hunted look. His breathing becomes normal. He starts to talk more freely to the boys, and later, when he sees they are still afraid of him, he becomes more authoritative.

Paul has no way of knowing that the transition in him was brought about by the influence of his environment. The environment never said to Paul, "From now on, you can bully these boys. They are afraid of you." It never talks. Its ways are the most subtle on earth. It is not even a whisper or a shadow. It speaks without speaking. It grows in you as the grass grows, soundlessly.

Without knowing how it happened, Paul developed an appetite for money, easy money. He came to know certain types of people intimately. There was a fellow, for instance, who weighed three hundred pounds if he weighed one. When Paul shined his shoes, the big fellow couldn't see them because of his enormous belly. Paul laughingly thought it was just like an umbrella; you could hide under it and never get wet in a downpour, not in a thousand years.

He was fun, this guy Rudolpho. He liked to laugh, and Paul was fascinated watching the way that jelly started to shake, as if someone were tickling it from the inside. All that fat would suddenly jump into the air, as if it wanted to find a new place for itself right under Rudolpho's chins. Then it seemed to fall down to his very knees, then up again and down, up and down, as if it had a separate life of its own.

Rudolpho was in the numbers racket. He hated moving around to see all the people he had to see, so he began taking Paul with him to do the leg-work. Paul was willing because Rudolpho was generous. For a couple of hours' work he would give him one, two, sometimes three dollars, depending on his mood and intake.

Rudolpho lived on other fellows as a louse lives on living things, and he tried to chisel for himself on the side. His job was taking bets and paying out on the rare times that some lucky bastard hit the right number. But Rudolpho wasn't satisfied with his take, and slowly tried to build up a clientele for himself. He knew that if he got caught by the big fellows he might be taken for a ride, but thought that since he acted decently to the people he dealt with, they would never give him away.

But there is always a leak somewhere, and one day when Paul went to Rudolpho's two-room apartment on West 110th Street, he was surprised to see the door half open. Rudolpho was a very cautious man. He had a chain and two Yale locks on his door and he would never, not even for a second, leave it open. His door was in a dark hallway just off the stoop, in a half-empty, condemned house, a firetrap if there ever was one. He had lived there alone for many years, cooking and cleaning for himself. He lived in constant fear.

Paul felt uneasy, seeing that half-open door. He pushed it cautiously and called out, "Rudolpho, are you there?" There was no answer. The shades were down, and it was almost black in the room. Paul stepped in and called again, but at the same instant he saw Rudolpho sitting in the middle of the room at a table, staring at him.

"You bastard," Paul said out loud, laughing. "You wanted to scare me, didn't you?"

He went to the behemoth and started to give him a friendly poke in the ribs, but stopped, startled. He saw that the grin on that face was frozen. On the white shirt was a zig-zag of dried blood. Rudolpho was dead, all right, and the spectacle of him sitting there, looking at Paul with sightless eyes and grinning, was the most ghastly thing he had ever seen in his life.

Environment is only a part—a very large part, to be sure—of ready-made motivation. In fact, environment is like a big, comfortable bed, waiting for us the moment we are born.

However, as our mental horizon widens, our environment

becomes uncomfortable, but fear of the unknown still keeps us glued to the now-despised but familiar places.

Without environment, no one can create a living, three-dimensional character.

THE STORY OF AN UGLY MAN

This will be the story of an ugly man who killed because *he thought* he was ugly.

In the previous part, we were witnessing environment in action. Now motivation again will help environment and its twin brother, physical make-up, to mold, or rather twist, a human being into a grotesque shape.

The following is an excerpt from a local newspaper:

WIFE-KILLER SURRENDERS

MOST BRUTAL MURDER IN THE ANNALS OF OUR TIME

WIFE'S FACE UNRECOGNIZABLE

HE DID IT, HE CLAIMS, BECAUSE HE LOVED HER

"Guy Smith was arrested last night for the brutal murder of his beautiful wife, Anne. Mr. Smith's arrest came as a complete shock to the community. He was known as an even-tempered fair-minded citizen, member of the local Rotary Club and generous supporter of many worthy and charitable causes."

Then the paper went into the gory details of how they found Mrs. Smith's mutilated body, what time the murder occurred, how Mr. Smith surrendered to the police. He was calm, serene, police reported. The fact is that Mr. Smith called the police himself. Then, with the utmost self-possession, he sat down in a rocking-chair and waited for his arrest.

Smith was not only willing to admit the murder but explained to the astonished district attorney how he had planned to kill his wife. This confession made the murder a premeditated one and Smith a candidate for the electric chair.

According to the psychiatrist, Smith was absolutely sane and responsible for his act. They pointed out to him that he had the legal right not to answer any questions which might implicate him, but Smith almost eagerly volunteered to give all the information which would help him to be executed as quickly as possible. In prison he was not even downhearted. He was jovial, seemed absolutely relaxed, as if he had no care in the world

Why should a seemingly healthy person wish to die? The normal reaction is to evade punishment, even if one has committed a crime.

How did all this transformation come about? His physical make-up was a very strong motivation in making him morbidly sensitive. He wasn't deformed or disgustingly ugly. He was just not the type one would call good-looking. His face was shallow, his nose broken, and his eyes always looked inflamed.

No, he wasn't exactly ugly, but unfortunately he thought he was, and this conviction of his made him what he became: a killer.

This man Smith was a tolerably intelligent man, but when he compared himself to others the result was very disheartening. His hypersensitivity and his unruly imagination made him see things that weren't there.

Who knows our limitations better than ourselves? To know how little one knows is a bitter pill for a sensitive person to swallow. Smith knew how limited he was in his profession. He was an accountant, a freelancer. Furthermore, he was painfully aware that as a human specimen he could not, by any stretch of the imagination, be called an Adonis.

His constant fear of losing his beloved wife made him kowtow to her, which, after a while, made him actually repulsive to her. His politeness and his eagerness to please increased, if possible, instead of diminishing.

This self-abasement went so far that it gave Mrs. Smith physical anguish to be near him. He was good twenty-four hours a day, and his behavior made it harder for her to tolerate him. She planned to leave him. He, on the other hand, sensing that his value was decreasing at an alarming rate, desperately tried to recoup the esteem he had lost through the years.

He began giving her expensive gifts, which he could not afford until he started accepting bribes to falsify income tax returns. He tried to transform himself from a middle-aged man into a young, vivacious one. He started to prance around, flirting with young women, making himself utterly ridiculous. His plan to make his wife jealous was so transparent that instead of being angry she actually encouraged his escapades, thinking that perhaps this way she could get rid of him sooner.

His expensive gifts were not appreciated. His wife felt an even greater need to escape. The tension grew between them, yet neither uttered a word about what was uppermost in their minds. The unbearable atmosphere had to explode, shattering all the make-believe, lies, and hypocrisy.

At last the truth came out—she wanted a divorce. And for the first time Smith consciously was pushed toward murder. For the first time he thought his wife should be dead. This thought was not born of frenzy. It was a logical step and he, in horror, was repelled by it almost the moment it was born. In the first split second that this idea came into being he knew that with her death he must die too. And he was not ready for that ultimate decision—yet.

The idea of killing someone is much more satisfying than that of seeing oneself as a corpse. This understandable love of life makes cowards of us all. Smith tried to figure out how he could stay alive. In his desperation he lost the last shred of human dignity. He begged, he threatened. Nothing mattered any more. He fought only for the humiliating privilege of being near her.

Did she allow it? She did, for various reasons. First, she really pitied him. Still another reason: since she told him that living with him was out of the question, she felt free to go out with other men, hoping Smith would reconcile himself to the inevitable.

And the most important reason of all: before leaving him she intended to collect half the price of their home—a six-family house in which she was part owner.

Smith was originally a kind, mellow man. The thought of murder must have grown slowly in his head. What kind of provocation must have exploded in his mind to have forced him to make that last fatal step, which ended not only his victim's life but his own?

Smith had asked only one privilege, that she let him stay. Feeling sorry for him she agreed, and with this act she started a chain of reactions which culminated in her death.

Again, the provocation must have been great. Strange men would come to *his* house. This was betrayal in his eyes. What right had she to defile his house?

Perhaps she never entertained the idea of bringing men into the house, but her actions may have suggested that she did.

He felt he could not go on thinking these thoughts. It was worse than the punishment promised to the blackest sinner in hell. But still he hoped she would come back to him. Why?

How in heaven's name would a man like Smith think, even for a moment, that everything might turn out for the best? Was there any possibility of this? None at all. Then why did he delude himself with false hopes? For a very good reason! This hope must have meant more to him than marital happiness—more than anything in the world. *It meant his life.*

This woman, when she met him, had made him believe that he *belonged: that he was as good as anyone else or better.* She made him believe in human dignity. She gave him the all-important feeling that he was wanted, that he was important, really important, and now she was ready to destroy all of the self-confidence she had built up in him.

This catastrophe had to be prevented at all costs. To him, her desire to leave meant deceit, betrayal. When they first met, she had lied to him about his prowess and his looks. Now a divorce would certainly make him the laughing-stock of all who knew him.

Divorce had much more significance to him than to others. It meant, in this case, that he would be left unprotected in the midst of a hostile world. Divorce meant losing the one thing that kept him alive—the security of marriage.

If she had lied to him when she said he was good, then his own previous estimate of himself was correct, and later it was conclusively proved that he was an inferior person who had no right to live.

Mrs. Smith's request for a divorce at this stage was to him tantamount to a polite announcement, "Look, Smith, you have lived enough; it is time that you lie down peacefully and die."

A divorce meant death to Smith. That is why he became desperate. He fought for his life, and when he lost hope of saving it, he killed—in self-defense, according to his topsy-turvy reasoning.

Smith was not insane. I would not be interested in him if he were. But I become increasingly excited as I observe him sliding irrevocably into desperation and chaos.

Whether one has a physical handicap or not, the important

thing is what the individual thinks of himself. If he feels he is not exactly a bargain, it is very hard to make him think otherwise.

The second most important motivation for human behavior is our own physical make-up.

Without experiencing in childhood humiliation, neglect, and abuse, or love and tenderness, no person can be a totally distressing pessimist or a smiling optimist.

A three-dimensional human being is not only influenced by his environment but by his physical make-up as well.

This man Smith must have had more than his share of humiliation in childhood to feel as he did about his looks.

Every living soul is eternally searching and fighting for security—the touchstone, the kernel, the important source of all human emotion and conflict.

Even the noblest of all human emotions, mother-love, springs from the knowledge that a woman's future life is insecure until her offspring are alive and propagate her kind to the end of time. Through her children a mother expects to achieve immortality, security even after death.

Bad judgment is not necessarily the result of ignorance, but if you put a case under scrutiny you will find that the person with bad judgment usually was ignorant of the subject concerning which he used his bad judgment.

A young woman of, say, twenty-five, works with a young man. She's good-looking, he's not. She has an almost perfect figure; he is paralyzed from the hips down. She's a stenographer, he's a young lawyer. They marry. The fact is, she proposed marriage and chased after him, and not he after her. Why?

For your information, here are the facts. The man was a young, struggling lawyer without any money whatsoever, and a cripple to boot. Why did she choose him for marriage instead of waiting for a healthy man with a more substantial background? Why? What was her motivation? From a distance it seems that her action was against all common sense. She was not in love with him, so what in Heaven's name was her reason?

Here is the motivation. The girl came from a very religious and conservative family. She had a widowed mother who worked hard to earn a living and support her only child. She took in washing and their two-room apartment was in perpetual confusion. Wet and drying clothes hung all over the place. According to her standards even to talk about sex was evil; to practice it without marriage would bring eternal hell-fire to the sinner. The girl, to escape this monotony, poverty, and ignorance, did have affairs, first with one, then with many other men.

It was a desperate revolt against her drab life. She felt guilty and remorseful but she had no strength to stop. Life offered very little to her. She managed to finish high school without learning much. She was a good girl, really. She loved and helped her mother, but only through her secret excursions into sex relationships with men could she keep her sanity.

When she met the cripple in the office his unashamed admiration for her made her decide to marry him. She believed that a normal man would never forgive her indiscretions, while this one would be happy just to have her as his wife. She knew she would be secure with him, that he would worship her.

There's your motivation.

Ask your friend why he married his wife. Or ask the wife why she married your friend. They may look at you with a smile and with great condescension say: "Because we loved each other." But ask them further: What is love? Oh no, they won't be embarrassed because, you see, they know all the answers, as most people do, and they will give you the bromide—love is a physical and spiritual attraction. People have heard this question and answer so often that they repeat it without questioning its validity.

If you want to understand motivation and want to write good stories or plays, you had better reject such insipid surface explanations. Love is much more than physical or mental attraction. It is more than compatibility—although these are part of the whole. Love is my firm belief that my beloved is absolutely devoted to me and this devotion gives me confidence in myself and in my future. I want to emphasize this point. Physical attraction plus compatibility plus the importance of being important plus the belief in this person's absolute loyalty add up to love; in short, love is security.

No, you don't have to accept my definition of love, or of anything else. You can formulate your own definition. You should anyway. You might as well know that rejection of a theory you disagree with is, if nothing else, a sign that your imagination is in working order. But remember that there is no guarantee that imagination will always carry you in the right direction. Slavish acceptance of tradition just because it is ancient can be as harmful as misdirected imagination.

Some writers just waddle along like a fat goose on top of a manure heap, pecking industriously away for some thought-morsels someone dropped carelessly. Such writing necessarily shows poverty of mind. Such an author kills a wife in his story because of a great discovery: the husband was jealous. You can look in vain for the host of motivations that swarm around, and for that which started the chain of events which at the end culminated in murder.

The new girl in the office was delighted with the woman office manager, who turned out to be not only charming but encouraging, and actually helped her to do her job in the proper way. She was surprised. She thought there must be a catch somewhere. No superior had ever been as solicitous as this one. The office manager was young, about twenty-eight, very good-looking, and had poise and good manners. Everyone loved her—including the two bosses. In fact, the younger one was "going after" her full blast. Why, then, her humility? Why wasn't she swell-headed as the managers in other offices usually were?

The new girl was very much intrigued with this strange behavior. Why did she behave as she did? Why all this goodness? And this woman's attitude toward all the personnel in the office wasn't just a passing fancy, she found out. Girls who had worked for her for years assured her that she was always the same.

Why? Here is the answer.

When she was eighteen she had been caught with her parents and two brothers in a fiery inferno as their house burned down. The four others died a horrible death. The doctors considered it a miracle that she remained alive. She lived and with much plastic surgery became once more a presentable young woman who could go out and earn her living. There are always exceptions, but most of those who have come into such close proximity to death as she did learn to look at life differently from those whose lives have not been marred with horror.

Since I am talking about motivation, this brings to my mind the curious phenomenon of a man who was a coward one day, and a death-defying hero the next. I wondered what could have made him act that way.

Cowardice, as I see it, is not a permanent state. It changes with circumstances and with the moods these circumstances create. A man may walk down the street not thinking of anything special. Suddenly he sees a woman crossing the street directly in the path of a speeding truck. The driver apparently doesn't see the woman, and the woman, deep in thought, doesn't hear the rumbling of the deadly monster rushing toward her.

There is no time for deliberation. He may spring forward under an impulse and pull the woman out of the way—although he may be crushed instead.

The time between recognizing the situation and deciding whether he should help the woman or not might require no more than a fraction of a second, but a thousand pictures of his past and present life will flash through his mind with the rapidity of lightning. In this infinitesimal time it will be decided whether this man will act in a cowardly fashion or heroically.

What causes him to feel ready to risk exchanging his life for that of an unknown person?

Scientists say that before the uranium atom splits, it first turns into plutonium. In the case of our man, no matter which decision he makes, a preliminary mood must be created. And in such an emergency it must happen swiftly. The material must be in him, ready to explode or fizzle out. What is the mood? What are the ingredients which have the power to overwhelm him to such an extent that in his "mood of exaltation" he is suddenly ready to sacrifice his life—when at other times he is just a plain, ordinary coward?

What is the definition of cowardice? The Century Dictionary says: "Cowardice: want of courage to face danger, difficulty, opposition; dread of exposure to harm or pain of any kind."

Accepting this as correct, we ask why this man should create a mood for himself which will make him brave and, in consequence, possibly cause his own death. The answer is that he is powerless to create any kind of mood. The ingredients in him decide the result beforehand; necessarily it must have been in him to start with. He has nothing to do with the final decision.

If he happened to have a mother who, for some reason or other, neglected him in childhood, he might have grown into adulthood with a bitter taste in his mouth against women. And if, to top this, he had had an unfortunate love affair, was betrayed, perhaps, his resentment might have grown to such proportions that he later married for one unconscious, single purpose—to take revenge on the sex which had humiliated him and made him feel unimportant.

The above conjecture might be only one of the many reasons that, while not deliberately making him condemn that woman to die before the onrushing truck, yet might make him hesitate for the split-second longer that would spell death to her.

Remembered experiences from the past will create a predetermined reaction and these, in the final analysis, will decide whether he'll appear a coward or a hero to those witnessing that particular scene.

The man who acts like a coward today may be a shining example of bravery tomorrow, for some other reason.

Motivation not only fascinates us but it is the very essence of all great writing. Nothing ever happened or ever will happen without sound motivation.

What a miraculous spectacle it is to see the blood on its tireless, unending travel under our skin, carrying oxygen through the entire body. But to show through your imagination and motivation how a pregnant thought can grow into determination, how determination crystalizes into action, is as miraculous as anything human ingenuity ever produced.

To motivate is to instigate; to incite to action; to induce to reason; to stimulate. Motivation can spring from many sources. One can be inspired by love, or spurred to action by hate; fanaticism will move one even to sacrifice one's life. Love for fame or for wealth are powerful instigators for action.

The basic source of all human emotion and all conflict is the eternal unquenchable thirst for security—in short, for self-preservation.

MAN OF GOD

Let me suppose that I see a jumble of headlines on the front page of my daily newspaper. I wonder which of the headlines will have the greatest attraction for readers. . . .

GEORGE MCCARTHY, 60, ELOPES WITH TEEN-AGER. Since I know myself better than anyone else I would, mentally at least, shake my head and say, "The damned old fool!" and read on, scanning the other headlines to find what might interest me more than an idiot who married a young girl.

MR. P., COMPTROLLER OF X. CORPORATION, ORDERED BY JUDGE . . . "Who cares?" NINETEEN NEW NATIONS ADMITTED INTO UNITED NATIONS . . . "Nice, very nice!" I nod with approval. ELECTRICAL WORKERS ON STRIKE . . . "Good Lord—now our bills will be higher again!" MRS. GILBERT SAND SHOOTS SLEEPING HUSBAND . . . "The bitch!" I cry noiselessly, and with a silent prayer I hope that my little woman will never do that to me (not in my sleep, anyway); on second thought, I am absolutely sure she would not, because she is not the type.

DEACON DESERTS FAMILY FOR CHOIR GIRL, 15! John Smith, deacon of Holy Saints Church, a devout believer in the Scriptures, father of seven children, runs off with a fifteen-year-old girl, a singer in the church choir.

I am sure that other readers, like myself, will take time to read this story, which promises to be exciting. A deacon of a church! Boy oh boy! A father of seven children. You silently say, shaking your head, "The old hypocrite! You can't trust anyone anymore." You may go on reading other headlines, but your mind will come back to John Smith, I am sure.

Why? The first headline was about McCarthy, an ordinary human being, but the deacon of a church is not. He is special.

Why is he so special? First of all, to sin is a common occurrence among ordinary people; the mortal flesh lives ready for perdition. But it is hard to believe that a superior man, like a man of science or a preacher of the gospel, is not made out of finer clay than ourselves.

I am a sinner, but I would lose faith in mankind if I could not find a nobler man than myself. So a deacon who, preaching God's Laws, forgets the most elementary rule of decent living, leaving behind a wife and innocent children, commits an even greater outrage than murder. This man Smith, because of his actions, destroys hundreds and thousands of families' trust in themselves and in their fellow men.

I am interested in this story and I want to probe further. Was John Smith a contemptible hypocrite? I find that he was not. He was fanatical in his religious zeal, the Holy Terror of the small town where he lived.

He was like an avenging angel to all who showed the slightest inclination to stray from the tenets of their faith. Many a woman had reminded her erring husband of the saintly John Smith, beseeching him to follow this shining example.

I learn that he is forty-nine years old, tall, very lanky and might once have been a handsome man but for his pock-marked face. He had rather distinctive light blue eyes of great intensity. Many people remarked that his eyes had an unusual power of which he could be proud. He frequently looked in the mirror to see what was so unusual about them, but he could never discover anything special. The fact is that he was puzzled about his eyes and he disliked them. He often thought them colorless and watery.

When he was young he helped out in his father's store, but he was very unhappy about it. The store was dark and dingy; the merchandise was haphazardly thrown about on the counters in a crazy jumble. If this was good enough for the Senior John Smith, it should also be good enough for Junior.

John Smith, Jr., in his youth was a very shy person. His pock-marked face looked repulsive to him and he thought that it was repulsive to others. In high school the attractive girls who were his schoolmates dated others, but they always politely turned him down. His appearance was the least of the reasons that the girls refused to be seen with him. To put it simply, he was below-average in intelligence.

He thought that the teachers hated him for some unknown reason and purposely gave him the most difficult problems to solve. He was bitter, and since he was healthy and physically robust, he antagonized his teachers and fought his classmates over the slightest misunderstanding. The other boys found him a dangerous adversary and left him strictly alone.

He slowly withdrew into himself. He had been attending church every Sunday, but now he started to listen to the lectures with great concentration. He liked to hear about a better world where the Good will go and be loved by God for all eternity. At this same time he started to take more interest in the store, where he worked after school, and for the first time he found that his father, instead of scolding him, found words for praising him. But the transaction from youth to maturity was not simple.

He could not absorb his lessons in school and was not promoted. He felt acutely the embarrassment of towering like a giant among the younger girls and boys in his class. He looked more like a grown man than a student.

Not long before his graduation he walked up to an attractive girl, a classmate of his, and started to talk to her. She was embarrassed to be seen with this backward boy but, being a sensitive young thing, could not insult him by refusing to walk home with him. As they passed through a deserted street, John suddenly grabbed the girl and started to rip her blouse open. The shocked girl was so stunned by this unexpected attack that she was petrified and unable to move to defend herself.

For the first time he could remember, he saw the bare breast of a woman. The small but firm shapes, with the rosy nipples, almost drove him into such madness as to make him rape her on the spot. He felt the heat of her body penetrate through his hands to his very bones. His eyes blurred. He was about to attack her when he thought he saw a blinding flash of light and heard the words, "Leave the girl alone!"

He knew then that it was God Himself, saving him from committing a hideous crime. He recoiled and started to back away from her, babbling incoherently, "No ... No ... No ... I did not mean that—please forgive me . . ." and ran away, crying and throwing wild words into the air.

At last, breathing heavily, he slowed down to a trot, and then to a walk, staggering as if he were drunk. He made sucking noises with his mouth, and looked back from time to see if someone was following him. When he saw a policeman ahead, he hid in a doorway. When he finally arrived home he was delirious. His mother immediately called a doctor but John closed his bedroom door and refused to open it. He was lying in bed with his clothes still on. He could still see the beautiful, tantalizing bare flesh of the young girl. He wanted to touch her flesh again and his fingers tore into the pillows.

He was genuinely sick and stayed in bed for weeks. He was ashamed to re-enter his life as if nothing had happened. He was also afraid that he might be arrested, and, as remorse convulsed him, he began to feel sorry for his father. He was sure that if his father should find out what had happened the shame would kill him. It was unthinkable that the girl had not reported the horrible incident. John was really sorry for that shameful episode, but the memory of the girl's nakedness remained vivid.

Later, when he went back to school, the girl was there, but she never gave even the slightest indication that anything had happened between them.

Young John Smith lived in mortal fear, driven by his guilt. He asked forgiveness of God, and he believed that the terrible burden of his abominable act slowly became lightened by the merciful God. His religious fervor became so satisfying that he felt happier than ever before in his life.

He decided that during all of his life God had been testing him. His repentance was so pleasing to his Maker that the feeling of guilt was slowly evaporating from his heart. At the age of twenty-five he started to study the Bible in earnest. He thought that he understood the Bible better than his own father, who was quite maniacal about it. They had feverish arguments, interpreting incidents in it according to their own understanding. He spent more and more time in church doing things that others left undone.

One day, in a blinding revelation, he suddenly saw the multitude of people in the streets, neglecting their immortal souls. He stopped still in the main square of the town and started to talk about salvation. He described the eternal joy of the believer in Jesus. He became so overwhelmed with his own fervor that he almost fainted under the compelling power of his own oratory.

John Smith was on his way, facing his destiny. He had found his mission in life; he saw with absolute certainty the goal of his life; he knew at last where he belonged. He had chosen God. Of course he had trouble with the church. The elders forbade him to make a spectacle of himself as he was not an accredited speaker for the church and they claimed that his irresponsible statements brought disgrace rather than honor.

John Smith, Sr., passed away and young John took over the store. Since he was happy only when he was preaching before a crowd, he rented an empty store nearby, obtained a permit to preach, and in no time had a large following. He was hard, as adamant as one can be, toward organized religion, driven by a deep-rooted hatred of those who had treated him as their inferior.

A few years passed by, and among his faithful followers he found Miss Clara Moriarity, a big-bosomed young woman approaching thirty. Clara Moriarity had seen life in the raw, sleeping with many men, in different beds. She was a waitress and, because of the treasure-house of her rich experience, she came to the conclusion that John Smith was probably the only man living who would be faithful to her. She therefore decided to marry him.

She attached herself to him with the idea that she would be a modern Magdalene. She became his shadow. One night she confessed some of her sins to him and he, in turn, embraced her with the understanding and love of a forgiving father.

A few days later, he asked her to marry him. She, in turn, begged him to give her a day to think it over. He did this gladly, but Clara was afraid that by the next day he might also think it over, or forget that he had ever proposed to her. However, she really needed that day to get rid of a ruffian named Pete, who had been coming to see her whenever the spirit moved him.

Clara and John were married and—miracle of miracles—Clara became a faithful and dutiful wife and mother. Those who had known her in former times thought that John Smith must have been a hell of a good lover to limit her insatiable female appetite to one man. Whatever the reason for her fidelity, the children that came year after year must have contributed a great deal to tying her down.

I have no desire to trace John Smith's tortuous road to sainthood. In short, however, his name became a by-word for decency and high moral standards. He also prospered in his business and turned any surplus over to charity for those who deserved help the most. He organized a choir that was accompanied by trumpets, and they made quite a stir whenever they appeared on a busy street corner.

One day John found a mousey little girl in his choir group who had two given names—Harmony-Olivia. She was not more than fifteen years old, the daughter of a crippled father and a mother who could hardly move because of advanced arthritis. The poor child was always hungry and somehow one day John noticed her eyes as she watched a girl in the choir who was eating a sandwich. His heart went out to this miserable creature. He took her hand and without explaining anything brought her home to Clara to feed.

Clara was angry. She claimed that she had enough hungry mouths to feed on the pittance he gave her for the table. John was not in the habit of arguing with his wife at any time. He just looked at her. On such occasions his watery blue eyes miraculously darkened, and there appeared in them a murderous fire. She kept quiet then and did what she was asked to do.

Clara had never forgotten her own miserable childhood. Since girlhood she had been driven from job to job, from city to city, looking desperately for a place where she could stop running. She had become very tired when she found John Smith and realized that this man could be her salvation. She could never forget to be grateful, and often compared this decent, God-fearing man with those selfish men in her life who only used her for their pleasure and left her without a second thought when they had had their fill.

Harmony-Olivia became a frequent guest in John Smith's house—in fact she became a very useful member of the household, helping with dishes and the hundreds of other small chores around the house. She followed him like a faithful dog. He was her personal god.

She brought food packages home to her parents and they, too, felt some peace of heart because she was protected from hunger by this godly man. They could never stop admiring him and they prayed fervently for his immortal soul.

John Smith, the evangelist, had one great sorrow in his so-far blessed life. All of his children were boys. Not one little daughter, not one lovely little girl-child ever clambered onto his lap and threw her tender little arms around his neck. He craved tenderness, and his family, instead of loving him, were actually a little in awe of him because they saw him so often at the service, haranguing and throwing angry Biblical quotations at the heads of the congregation before him, threatening them with hell-fire and damnation if they did not live up to the Scriptures.

John Smith, with all his worshipping crowd around him, was a very lonely man, and there was no one to whom he could unburden his heart.

The time came when Clara was always fidgety and nervous. It did not occur to John that his abstinence from sexual relations with Clara might have made her edgy. She had had her share of conjugal bliss, but for two years now since she had become pregnant with her youngest child he had explained to her, as kindly as he could, that he had no desire to bring forth more children into this suffering world and it would be sinful to continue their sexual relationship.

Clara had been angry for the first time in their fifteen years of marriage. She had argued that it was her right to sleep with her lawful wedded husband, but he was adamant. Clara, therefore, had lately begun to have very inflammatory dreams which left her limp and tired the next morning. She was tempted to take a lover, but was afraid.

Little Harmony-Olivia's help became more and more important around the house. In fact, she worked so late that it became dangerous to let her go home alone to the old tenement where she lived. So she moved in and became one of the family.

I am stopping here to evaluate what I have done so far. A man need not have a face covered with pockmarks to feel inferior. There is no man on earth who does not feel subconsciously that there is something vital missing from his make-up. Inferiority manifests itself in a million different ways. I think John Smith would regard his disfigured face as a handicap and ignore his mental deficiency.

He turned to religion not necessarily because he was intellectually limited but because religion was around him in his home environment and easy for him to use to his advantage. He was as strong as a bull and brutal enough when he decided to go after what he wanted. He believed implicitly in his own faith, and had sublime confidence in himself through his conviction that whatever he wanted was approved by God.

A strong man who has acted independently for many years and suffered no catastrophic consequences will become convinced that his decisions are always right.

This man, then, is one who must develop from Pole One, which in his case is respectability, even nobility, to Pole Two, dishonor. The step-by-step transition, or trans-polarization, is considered by professional writers the most difficult part of creating in words.

Let me show you how John Smith goes from decency to dishonor—but I must warn you that the following transition is not the only one possible. The interpretation of a character depends on the individual writer's intelligence and imagination, his personal philosophy, and even his blood pressure! No two people will ever interpret a subject in exactly the same way. A fictional character's growth will be influenced by the talent and character of the writer.

Now if the background I drew for John Smith is a good one, I can trace his psychological growth.

As a child he fought with his classmates and teachers and then withdrew into his own thoughts. What these thoughts were, as more and more he moved into adolescence, are not hard to surmise. Nature saw to it that he thought about sex; his lack of friends kept him from the speculations, bull-sessions, explorations, and substitute athletics which supply a measure of relief to the boy who is accepted by his group.

By the time he was a young man, though still in high school, his sexual desires were a constant torment, increased by pornography found in used-book stores, masturbation followed by guilt, and his own fervid imaginings. When he found himself alone with a young girl for the first time, his control slipped. Fortunately, a combination of circumstances sent him rushing away from her so that rape was averted. Surprise at his own behavior, combined with the girl's obvious terror, the fact that they were outdoors and it was only afternoon, and the nervous shock that he later interpreted as the voice of God threw him into reverse, so to speak.

The nervous illness that followed gave him plenty of time to consider not only the excitement of sex but the grim results if one is caught taking it by force. Remember, he can't imagine a woman wanting him; to enjoy sexual activity with a woman he must risk the punishing disapproval of God and man. His deep desire is for admiration, not loathing.

Ashamed, afraid, he accompanied his family to church as was customary, but at last he found a ray of hope. He directed all his thoughts and emotions toward religion, and sure enough, his guilty terror slowly diminished. Religious fervor replaced sexual fervor. Moreover, this was the time in his life when he was through with the frustrations of high school. Working in the store brought approval from his father, and working in the church brought approval from the community. John had achieved some importance, and he was able to fight the hungers of the flesh which might wreck his new status until he was twenty-nine—and a complete celibate.

Then Clara came along. He was excited by her obvious sensuality and might well have rejected her had she not had balancing qualities for him. For one thing, she was a repentant sinner who worshipped him; how could a godly man turn from a Magdalene? For another thing, she made no secret of her desire to marry him; his pockmarks in no way repelled her.

With the sanction of the church, John indulged in his lust for his wife until they had had seven children. The wild excitement of the first months of marriage had not lasted once sexual release became a matter of course for him, but it wasn't until the birth of the seventh child that John knew he was sick of his wife.

Clara was recuperating from childbirth. John had not gone to bed with her for several weeks. When the older children were born, he had felt his deprivation keenly and increased his prayers until he could resume the marital relationship. This time, however, he had felt fine—full of energy, spiritually clean. He had seen Harmony-Olivia in the choir and paid no special attention to her before; now she seemed to him the purest, holiest, most virginal creature in the world. He spoke to her and her shy adoration made him feel closer to his God.

He realized that he didn't think about God at all when he was with Clara. She had appealed to the bestiality in him. Why, when he came to think of it, her sinful past had undoubtedly taught her tricks to quicken the desires of the innocent male. The very thought of returning to her bed was repulsive and, when Clara eventually made an issue of it, he announced the termination of their sexual relationship on the purest of religious bases.

Even after Harmony-Olivia was living in his home as mother's helper, John's thoughts of her were aesthetic. She was a thin, timid child who made him feel saintly. Not even

the much-put-on Clara considered her a rival. But one particularly humid summer night, John wandered through the
house unable to sleep. Harmony lay on the living-room
couch, which served as her bed. She was asleep, naked above
the waist. Her virginal breasts smiled up at him like white
flowers. Suddenly he began to cry and ran out of the room.

For days thereafter he relived the experience. Harmony
was so maddeningly different from the ripe Clara in every
way; she was young and pure, and she was beyond sin.

One day John Smith found himself quite alone in the
house with Harmony and, overwhelmed by her presence and
her submissiveness, asked her if she was happy to be near
him. Harmony burst into tears as she replied haltingly that
he had given her heaven on earth, and that from now on,
and always, her life belonged to him.

Slowly and gently he embraced the loving little girl and, at
the moment that he touched her, he experienced a sensation
he had never dreamed existed. In turn, Harmony-Olivia, the
unspoiled little virgin, when she felt his strong arms around
her, sprang to life, threw both arms around his neck and
clung to him with an iron grip. Her little body melted into
his, and they stood transfixed.

Clara happened to come into the room just then, and for a
moment she just stood there, looking as if she had been mes-
merized. Then, with a hoarse bellow she gripped Harmony's
yellow hair and yanked her away from John with such force
that Harmony hit the floor with a heavy thud and lay there as
if dead.

John threw himself to his knees and started to lift the half-
conscious girl in his arms. "Monster!" he cried, facing Clara
with naked hatred in his eyes. But Clara could not be shaken
off with a sharp word. She bent down and tore at Harmony,
pummeling her. Harmony regained consciousness and ran
out of the house to save her life.

I shall stop here and see what possibilities I have here to further develop my story. (1) John subdues Clara and lets Harmony escape. (2) Another possibility—that John, in his fury, might pick up some heavy object and with one savage blow split Clara's skull. I select the first possibility and let Harmony escape because it offers more.

Harmony escapes, and Clara and John, after a terrific row, make peace for the time being. But Clara suspects that John is deceiving her with Harmony and she threatens him with exposure if he does not leave that young hussy alone.

If he were to have killed her in his outburst of anger the story would have been finished. But with Harmony escaped, and John intimidated by threats of exposure, I've created suspense wondering what he will do next. Clara watches his every move while he—spouting the Scriptures—threatens all sinners with hell-fire and damnation! Evangelists of this type always have an angry, unforgiving God behind them.

Clara hounds Harmony and her miserable parents, threatening them with exposure. They are ready to leave town, but when John realized what has been happening, he is forced to make a quick decision. For fear he might kill Clara in another overheated argument, he elopes with Harmony.

DEACON RUNS AWAY WITH A FIFTEEN-YEAR-OLD-GIRL, the headlines shriek. John Smith was a violent man and his end would be violent also. He escapes with the girl, and under the disguise that he is traveling with his daughter, they actually live together as man and wife.

He keeps her in bondage, hides her, and tyrannizes her, becoming fearfully jealous. Harmony at last sees that her god has feet of clay and wants to go back to her mother. John knows that if she escapes from him he cannot watch her twenty-four hours of the day. He implores her to stay with him, but Harmony's mind is made up and she insists she wants to go home. John knows, of course, that she can go home, but not he—not even if Clara would be willing to forgive him. He knows many of his followers would never forget. John and Harmony wrangle for days until, in a violent quarrel, he kills her, walks into the police station and gives himself up.

In a sketchy way this shows the inevitable end of a man who was possessed more by sex than love of God. John Smith, the protagonist, was ruthless enough to force conflict throughout, to the bitter end. This conflict stems from his uncompromising attitude, his suppressed desires and, above all, his real fear of sex, which had culminated in that shameful attack on an innocent schoolmate, throwing him into a religious frenzy. The remorse over this unfortunate act had kept him a celibate to the ripe old age of twenty-nine, when he met the voluptuous Clara, who had affected him with such force that even her confession about her past brought compassion and, at last, hope for fulfillment.

Magdalene of the Bible must have played an important part in his impressionable mind, and he had compared himself with Jesus, who had also forgiven these sins. This mental state was logical enough to fall into a pattern necessitating conflict. The resolution of murder is inevitable.

Harmony's saintliness so overwhelmed John that he could not extricate himself from his bondage. For John, to defend the helpless Harmony became an act of sacred duty; she was to him a saint and innocence incarnate. Always fanatical about everything, Harmony became so important to him that he imagined that he was defending not a woman but a symbol of God.

John Smith was no better, or worse, than any of us. He interpreted happenings according to his own understanding, and naturally tried to show his acts in the best possible light. I do not believe for a moment that he was a hypocrite. He was, rather, a fanatic who believed that everything he did was just. This is just one version of John Smith, but of course there may be other versions.

You might show him not as a fanatic but as a true hypocrite, whose clandestine affair with Harmony corrupts not only the girl but her parents and everyone around them. Since such deceit can seldom be kept secret for long, a widening circle of acquaintances would become aware of his defections. The whole situation would be thrown into the open one day, and his followers, in their righteous indignation, would force him to leave town.

Still another version would be his having an affair with Harmony, who is not saintly but conniving for her own ends, and wishes to be his wife. She becomes pregnant and demands that he get a divorce from Clara. Of course John knows that Clara would never agree to this. This version would also open up many unholy roads that would carry John to his own destruction.

Now let's look at the growth and transition. John is caught up in the web of his own contradictions, and it is vital for him to extricate himself if he does not want to be destroyed. The ensuing struggle creates a rising conflict.

THE GENEROUS MAN

I suppose people would be justified in wondering why a jealous man behaves like an idiot when actually there is no valid reason for his jealousy. But very few people would ask the seemingly stupid question as to really why a generous man is generous. People think the answer is simple: a man is generous because he is understanding, kind, and loving.

We would say happily Amen, and add that, in a nutshell, a generous man is generous because he is good. Period.

I'm sorry, but we can't dismiss this tremendous problem as simply as this. Of course, I'm not talking about people who have only occasional outbursts of generosity. Waiters and taxi drivers can tell which customer is a poor man and which is not because a poor man in such circumstances seeks to make an impression.

A generous man is different from the extravagant tipper. His generosity is not sporadic. It is as steady and uninterrupted as breathing. It is a principle with him. It is a sacred concept to live by.

Here is a case history. I've known this man and I am absolutely sure many of my readers know someone like him.

They called him good old Charlie. The funny thing is, he wasn't old and he wasn't Charlie.

He wasn't a day over forty and his name really was Edward, although no one used it except his family. He was six feet tall, bent a little, and his skin was grayish but no one noticed it because of the almost perpetual smile on his face.

He was the kindest man imaginable. He always had a good word for everyone and good old Charlie had never, not even once, complained that his friends could remember. It seemed his life was paved with contentment, peace, and happiness.

Nothing could have been further from the truth. His wife Maria was a fine, gentle woman but sickly. She lost patience easily but she never raised her voice or nagged him. She just looked. But in that look was compressed all the horror of Dante's Inferno.

The money Charlie earned was just enough to take care of their modest four-room apartment in the West Bronx and their two growing boys, Eddie, ten, and Paul, eight.

One Friday evening, pay-day, his wife Maria was in the living room, her blue-veined hands resting in her lap. She looked old and very tired.

CHARLIE (*enters with a cheery hello but Maria gives him only a tired stare*) : Anything wrong, dear?
MARIA: Have you got your pay?

CHARLIE (*with his usual exuberance*): A strange thing happened as I came up from the subway . . .

MARIA (*irritated*): I know. Someone was waiting for you. And in trouble, wasn't he?

CHARLIE: Now wait a minute! This is really a tragic case, Maria. I bumped into Dave . . .

MARIA: I know. They're all tragic cases. And they all need money.

CHARLIE: Are you being sarcastic, Maria?

MARIA: I'm too sick and tired to be sarcastic. How much did you give him?

CHARLIE: Why don't you listen first to what happened to him?

MARIA: I only care about what happens in this house. Today, for instance, I had no food to give the boys. I had to send them over to your Aunt Millie to be 'fed.

CHARLIE: For heaven's sake! You shouldn't have done that! Everybody will hear about it!

MARIA: What else could I do? How much is left of your pay?

CHARLIE: David's really had it hard this time.

MARIA (*not listening*): The store closes at six. Please give me whatever money you have. I've got to have food for dinner, Ed.

CHARLIE: Oh dear, you've just made up your mind not to listen.

MARIA (*with a sudden gasp*): You didn't give him . . . all?

CHARLIE: Don't be angry with me! His wife needs a serious operation immediately. It's a tumor. The doctor said that to postpone the operation would jeopardize her life!

MARIA: In short, you gave all your week's pay to Dave?

CHARLIE (*miserably*): You seem to think I did it purposely just to aggravate you.

MARIA: No, Ed. I'm sure David's wife needs that operation. Also there are countless other wives and kids who need

operations, or shoes and overcoats, or money to pay their
rent or buy food. That's it, Ed, food. You happen to have a
family, a nice family, I would say, but you go around helping everyone in the whole world but your own.

CHARLIE: You're very unfair. You're bitter, my dear. In my
place you would have done the same.

MARIA: No, Ed. I would think of my family first. Whenever
I hear someone telling me what a wonderful husband I
have, I want to say no, I have a very weak, miserable man
for a husband.

CHARLIE: Maria, what are you saying?

MARIA: The truth, Ed. The bitter truth. You're not good . . .
you are a coward. You want the whole world to think how
wonderful you are, and you're ready to sacrifice your wife
and children for this. (*angrily, shrilly*) What's wrong with
you? Why do you have to be so humble all the time? What
wrong have you done that you crave the approval of others
so much?

CHARLIE: I have never done a wrong thing in my life.

MARIA (*with a sigh of resignation*): I know. I fell in love
with you for that. A wonderful, good man. Real security, I
thought. A man who would always be loyal. But now . . .
I hate the sight of you. (*She stands up, ready to walk out.*)

CHARLIE (*frightened*) : Maria, please! People will hear you!

MARIA: I'm leaving you now, Ed, before we all starve to
death.

CHARLIE: Maria, I promise before the Almighty God, I'll
never again give a penny away. From now on I'll live only
for my family.

MARIA: You've promised once too often. I can't trust you any
more. (*She goes, but stops at door.*) Do you know that
except for your own family, everyone calls you Charlie?
They took away your name, your money, and now they'll
take away your wife and sons.

CHARLIE (*stops her*): I won't let you go, Maria. I love you too much! If you go away I might as well die. . . .

MARIA: All right then, tell me what is wrong with you, Charlie? What's wrong?

CHARLIE: Ed! Call me Ed! Please, Maria, don't humiliate me. My name is Ed.

MARIA (*looks at him pityingly*) : You came from a poor family—so did I, like millions of others, but we're not crawling. We stand on our own feet and fight back. What's wrong, Charlie? What's wrong with you?

CHARLIE: Don't call me Charlie. I won't allow anyone to call me Charlie from now on. I warn you, Maria.

MARIA: All right, you're not Charlie. But who are you then? Tell me, what makes you such a coward?

CHARLIE: I don't know. I never could be like others. I just love people, that's all—and it makes me happy when they love me.

MARIA: Everyone wants to be loved—but not as much as you do.

P.S.: The ending of this sketch is, of course, not conclusive. It would take years of abuse and ridicule for Charlie to reach the point of doing something rash. The above is merely a synopsis rather than gradual character growth.

It is more than possible that Ed, after years of soul-searching, might have died without knowing the real reason, the motivation, for his excessive generosity, which was so simple —he wanted to belong to the human race.

Or perhaps he realized that he hadn't any sort of talent that could make him an outstanding person, even just enough to be noticed, so he did what was the easiest thing for him—to try to please others and help them when they needed help.

People are eternally looking for someone on whose shoulder they can cry out their troubles—and Edward, the good old

Charlie that he was, found this pleasurable instead of tiresome. Somehow he always felt better after he had listened to other people's woes.

He was a real Samaritan. He knew when he did a good deed. But of course he never thought he was doing it because he wanted to be important. His metabolism seemed to work better and his blood pressure seemed just right whenever he helped people with money or with sympathetic advice. He actually lived to help. It became a necessity, like breathing. It might have been even more important to him than having sexual relations with his wife.

A man who craves recognition that much must be a lonely man, a man who, even if he is married, is not important enough to his wife or his children. Ed was not really lonely and he was loved, but over the years Maria soured because of the neglect resulting from her husband's preoccupation with helping others. Perhaps she was an extremely capable woman and Ed didn't feel that she needed him. Perhaps she made him feel inadequate. Whatever the reason, helping others was the only way he knew to be important before himself and before the world.

A writer getting hold of a character like Ed can write a play or a novel about his contradictions if he is truly three-dimensional. It is vitally important to remember that to change or even modify character is almost impossible because to give up generosity, for instance, would be to live without a purpose.

No one decides in his youth whether he really wants to be a hypocritical, a vindictive, or an over-generous man. There are inborn characteristics in all of us, and it depends on our physical make-up and our environment what direction we shall take in the future.

Motivation must be as evident in your creative writing as the nose on your face.

Motivation for man serves to build an enduring, all-em-

bracing edifice called importance for his safety. But the important façade is not immune to a constant bitter attack. Man, like the spider, is forced constantly to reinforce, to repair, even to rebuild his damaged edifice.

LOVE: THE FIRST STEP TOWARD SKEPTICISM

The young have no conception of what real love is. They love as they eat—by instinct. They need more security, much more, than grownups do. The young are like our ancestors were millenia ago, wandering upon the earth, crisscrossing tracks over territories, tasting fruits which might be poisonous. And had the fruits been poisonous, our ancestors might have died. If they had recovered, they would have been wiser for the experience.

The following is the first serious encounter of two youngsters with merciless reality. On the surface it seems to be a childish little affair—but it is not. It is full of sinister implications.

A girl of sixteen and a boy of nineteen sit in the girl's living room, petting. Her parents are at the theatre.

THE GIRL (*just for a moment comes up for breath; she can hardly talk*): John . . . now behave yourself. Wait . . . let me alone! Let me talk first. Do you really love me? Honest, do you?

THE BOY (*very excited, he considers her question immaterial and tries to resume his interrupted love-making*): Don't talk now.

THE GIRL (*considers the boy's actions ungentlemanly; demands an answer*) : You have to tell me. Do you love me? Oh, John. Please, John. Oh no! First tell me! (*She fights off another desperate attempt on the part of the boy to reach her.*) Not until you tell me. Do you? Do you?

THE BOY (*his determination to carry on undaunted is broken by the iron will of his adversary*): Okay, I love you! Are you satisfied?

THE GIRL: How much?

THE BOY: Now don't start that again! Don't be silly!

THE GIRL: I'm not silly. Say it. How much do you love me?

THE BOY (*wants to get it over with*): More than anything? Okay?

THE GIRL: What is anything?

THE BOY (*considers this last question of hers sheer cussedness but tries to answer, although he really doesn't know how*): Anything must be everything. Right?

THE GIRL: That's no answer. You don't want to tell me because you don't really love me.

THE BOY: Your folks will be home in no time. Don't waste time talking.

THE GIRL (*crying*): But I want to be sure. I want to hear it. You can't kiss me if you don't say it.

THE BOY: I love you, I love you, I love you! A million times I love you ... forever and ever and ...

THE GIRL *is at last convinced, now she knows she can be sure of his love, and with an upsurge of ecstasy clings to her young sweetheart.*

What does the above episode signify? Naked fear. Fear of the unknown is always with us. One feels the urge of awakening sex with conflicting emotions. Desire with fear throws girls into a dilemma. What will happen if? Do I miss something if I hold back? Am I a coward? What if I become pregnant? The decision is hard, especially for a teen-ager who has spent sleepless night after night imagining what every girl must experience sooner or later, until a strong, demanding male comes along and helps her to make a decision.

He will promise the sky, the world, the universe. His touch will make her blood run wild. She wants to believe, wants to be possessed, but what if . . . There are men who cannot be trusted, she has heard. She wishes to God he would take her against her wishes—the responsibility then would rest on him and not on her. She could stand being a victim instead of a person who wanted all this to happen to her.

But the boy relies on his eloquence to convince her that he would never hurt her; that he will stop whenever she wants him to. Just one kiss, a small little kiss can't harm her, can it? She admits it can't, and so opens the way for just a little kiss. She is kissed, but he will not stop there—he knew that beforehand, and she really hoped he wouldn't.

She is thrilled as her body is awakened, but panic grips her at the same time. What will happen to her after it's over? She feels she is in danger and pushes the man away, even though she's almost paralyzed. She wants her lover to be strong and persistent, yet when he is a feeling of guilt wells up in her. Can she trust him? Does he mean what he said? Fear ripples through her again and almost extinguishes her desire to experience the intoxicating feeling that only sex can give.

"Tell me you love me, love me!"

She is frantic to hear that he would do anything for her, even die for her, but he's too excited, too near the climax and can't think of a thing but his overwhelming emotions. She beats him or scratches his face just for a scrap of encouragement. Tell me you love me!

In a vision she sees what the future could hold for her: shame. She might become pregnant. She sees her mother's distorted face . . . her father's silent, accusing eye on her. What are her friends going to say?

All these and a million other horrors crowd her mind and make her force her lover to say things, endearing things, to her. She knows that the little words "I love you" of themselves really mean nothing, yet they give her the courage to go on, and make her forget her danger. For the first time she can exult in unleashed passion and experience the joy the poets sing about.

And after the first exultation, the first passion, she feels she belongs only to that one man for the rest of her life. She clings to him, the first man to know her so intimately. And at that very moment, when she could be the happiest person in existence, comes the cold, never-to-be-forgotten humiliation of her life.

She wants him to stay with her, to wait for her folks to come back, feeling that from now on her allegiance belongs not to her family but to this boy who has possessed her. And then he claims he must go. He's sorry but he cannot stay one moment longer. He must attend to a very important affair that cannot wait. It is annoying, he says, but he's sure she will understand because she is very intelligent.

She cries, she begs. Nothing can move him and he leaves. She has heard so much of man's inhumanity and infidelity and now at last she's confronted with it.

Let's suppose that he really has an important appointment. Still she feels their love-making was of such tremendous importance that it must supersede all else for the moment.

She has now made her first fundamental mistake concerning men. To him the occasion wasn't that important. He had experienced the same sensation many times before. He also knows he must be very careful with these silly creatures. They think if they let you make a little love to them, you belong for the rest of your life to that one girl. What nonsense! Run while the running is good.

One thing is certain: they are afraid of consequences just as the girls are. Another girl, who has already gone through such an experience, knows disappointment and, to a degree, humiliation, but she may feel that the competition is too keen and she must offer more to the man if she wants to keep him. Such rationalization will lead her to still more humiliation.

The girl who is left after her first experience feels she's been betrayed. She will not wait up for her parents to come home but in solitude, in her own bed, she'll relive her fearful and at the same time exciting experience—and with the great tolerance that only a woman has the capacity for, will try to understand her boy friend's hypocrisy and his transparent excuses as to why he had to leave so abruptly.

It is interesting to read an article by a noted psychiatrist, Frank S. Caprio, on "The Biology of Love." "Seven million American women," he writes, "admit they find sex unsatisfactory or even physically distasteful." No wonder, after such experiences.

Another noted psychiatrist, O. Spinger English, states: "One marriage in ten has a satisfactory sexual relationship." What a horrible picture that is!

A girl, in her innocence, takes it for granted that when she lets a man penetrate the sacredness of her body she can trust him forever. A crude awakening to reality will be hard to forget.

It is possible that such memories could ruin a marriage that is consummated many years later? Of course not. We never do a thing for one reason. Success or failure of a marriage never depends on one or two disappointing episodes. We should always first take into account all of our childhood memories; then the inherited characteristics, the mental or physical illnesses in the families, the broken homes, promiscuity, neglect, poverty, and many personal phobias of the people involved.

If one could eliminate painful experiences, it would not necessarily make a person happier.

Never experiencing an upset stomach or headache or any

kind of pain, or living without frustration would render a human being a freak, without compassion for others, and in the end he would die of a sickness of which he was never aware.

Disappointment, painful or not, is a necessary evil. One person will be wiser from it, while another will be crushed, never to recuperate from the blow.

Survival will depend on intelligence, perseverance, health, inherited characteristics, upbringing, and a good, healthy family life—but it would be a miracle if the aftermath of her first disastrous affair did not leave a girl with a healthy skepticism. Will such a dose of skepticism harm a young girl? Not at all. Just the opposite. Often it is the first step to maturity.

II

Young people don't know that their little game of mutual attraction is a trap that Nature devised to catch the unwary. Nature has no interest in whether the participants are intelligent or stupid, beautiful or ugly. Her goal is to make them cohabit in order to carry on the race.

Only Man has the capacity to reason, to plan, to foresee, while all other mammals instinctively select the strong or the beautiful to carry on their species.

Love is the gravitational force in orbit with life. Love is physical and mental attraction, plus emotional security.

Love includes begetting offspring and fighting for their safety. The sex urge is part, a very big part, of love; it is really the "life urge" camouflaged as sex, When the last shimmering desire for sex is snuffed out, that man is as good as dead.

Depending upon our physical and mental make-up, our idea of perfection shifts to conform to the latest excitement in our lives. A picture of an actress may impress us so strongly that our attachment to a previous ideal evaporates.

In *Romeo and Juliet,* Shakespeare demonstrates how

swiftly youth can change from complete worship of one person to adoration of another.

Romeo was so madly in love with Rosalinda that without hesitation he risked being killed when he attended the same party as she. Then he saw Juliet and, in the upsurge of new ecstasy, his great love for Rosalinda dissolved into thin air.

To adults this supersonic speed must seem ridiculous but in reality it is the most natural thing in the world. (Romeo was not more than sixteen.)

Youth goes through this kind of metamorphosis, from one state of mind to another, almost by the hour. Every little seemingly insignificant episode adds to or detracts from a precious concept of his life.

Of course the years of adolescence are considered the formative ones. However, the formative years never stop but merely slow down as we grow older. When we arrive at the ripe old age of twenty, our likes and dislikes are more or less formed. We claim that by now we are attracted only to a certain type of the opposite sex, but this "certain type" usually fluctuates according to place and circumstance.

So far we have not really arrived at an absolutely rigid stand, but there always is a day when all this happy philandering will be changed. Someone appears on our horizon and our search is abruptly terminated. We are going to feel with absolute certainty that the right person has at last arrived.

Why this should be the right one, the one and only who could make us sublimely happy, is not clear as yet, but the terrible need to be near this person is unmistakable.

The strange and almost grotesque thing in this affair is that the person who causes the blood in our veins to boil may not even remotely resemble the type we always professed to love before.

What could have happened?

What magic has this stranger wrought upon us to overcome our natural resistance?

Real love is not an overnight affair, when, after one or two disagreements all hell breaks loose and sobering disillusion follows. No, real love is made of much stronger stuff than that. When you find it you will feel that at last you have found a haven which will protect you even if all the calumnies of the world were to fall on your head.

Love is the most desirable, the most precious thing life can offer us.

How can we recognize real love which endures hardship? How does it look when it is genuine? The answer is that love is physical and mental attraction plus emotional security.

Many people will resent the statement that real love is based on security. If we ask them what *they* think love is, they have a ready answer.

"It is to give without ever thinking of security." Of course we might go overboard in giving without ever thinking of security, but when we do, it is because *subconsciously* we have been reassured that our love was appreciated and returned in kind.

Love, real love, is a conscious emotion; it is not a blind devotion. Real love rarely goes on the rocks, because the people involved know what to expect from each other. They aren't blind; they are aware of the pitfalls of being in love and are prepared for the best and for the worst.

Love has the magic power to make the lowest of men become the most important man in the world.

WHY WE FALL OUT OF LOVE

To discover the invisible nuances of the mind is the eternal quest for the creative writer. I hope this section will contribute useful observations to those interested in the subject.

Why do we fall out of love? What an idiotic question. Any fool can answer that one.

Reason one: nagging. Reason two: lack of appreciation. Reason three: being taken for granted. Reason four: wait . . . let's stop here. Being taken for granted seems to me the worst one. A friend of mine, a very nice gentleman, told me not long ago that he had a dream. The most awful dream a husband and father could have, especially if it is close to reality.

Here it is, as it was told to me. (It is strange that dreams always imitate Ionesco or Beckett or any of the daring men on the flying trapeze.)

A room with lots of wild kids running around, and a woman busying herself. A man unobtrusively sneaks into the room. (He is the father and husband.) Everyone is there but no one seems to see him. It is as if he were invisible. He walks on tiptoe, surreptitiously takes off his coat, sits down in a corner, and commences to wait. Meanwhile the children start to crawl all over him as if he were a piece of furniture and he acts exactly like a piece of furniture. Not a word out of him, no movement of any sort. Mother calls the children for supper. They eat, while the man still waits. He's the breadwinner, of course, the father of these brats and the faithful husband of this woman. Obviously they take him for granted. The man timidly indicates with his hands that he is hungry. Nobody notices him. The woman offers more and more to the children and finally what the children do not eat she scrapes into a bowl which she disdainfully throws before the man. He eats gratefully, hungrily, noiselessly. Slowly the wife and children disappear from the room, leaving the dirty dishes on the table, and the man who was taken for granted stands up, gathers the dirty dishes, washes them and puts them away, and then begins to make the bed. When he finishes making the bed he gets an old blanket, full of holes, puts it under the bed, and crawls after it. The wife enters,

takes off her clothes, climbs into bed and turns off the light.
There is a moment's silence.

HUSBAND (*from under the bed*) : Goodnight, dear. (*no answer; sotto voce as if praying*) The Lord is full of compas·sion and gracious; slow to anger and plenteous in mercy.

WIFE: Who's there?

HUSBAND (*from under the bed*): Your beloved husband. "Hear ye, Hear ye, for as the Heaven is high above the earth, great is His mercy towards them that fear him." I am cold here, Martha. (*He shivers so that the bed above him shakes.*)

WIFE (*cries out in anguish*): Nagging—always nagging! This mental cruelty is getting on my nerves.

HUSBAND: You used to allow me to sleep in bed once in a while. (*he shivers*)

WIFE (*irritated*) : Stop shivering—you worm!

HUSBAND: I'm sorry, dear! Martha, may I say something?

WIFE: No!

HUSBAND: I'm afraid you're taking me for granted.

WIFE: Always whining—always sorry for yourself.

HUSBAND: It's very cold here.

WIFE: Shut up!

HUSBAND: Yes, dear.

WIFE: I think the only solution to this misery of mine is a divorce. (*silence*) Why don't you answer? Didn't you hear what I said? (*no answer—she is getting angry*) Speak up, you miserable creature, when I'm speaking to you. (*Now she is infuriated—she jumps out of bed.*)

I'd better stop right here and let someone else finish this story. There could be as many endings as there are writers. You will find endless characters in the coming chapters all suffering the deadly malady of misunderstanding, incompatibility, indifference and imbecility.

Saltpeter, sulphur, and charcoal make gunpowder. Take any part of it away and the remainder is harmless. H_2O means water, the composition of hydrogen and oxygen. Leave out one or the other and that which was before is no more.

Love is possible because it is based on absolute trust, and trust means security against the whole hostile world.

But precisely how does one start to fall out of love? Does some great disappointment start the avalanche? Possibly. But more than likely the process was started by something small.

Disappointment or loss of confidence in a partner is enough to start a slow transformation which will result in mistrust, and mistrust is a sure sign that love has started to wither. The sorry fact is that many broken marriages were foredoomed even before the prospective partners laid eyes on each other.

People usually conceal their real characters during courtship. They are inclined to be more generous, more broadminded, more understanding and more tolerant, but six months or a year later the sweet tune of courtship no longer sounds so sweet. Confronted with the hardships of everyday living, the couple faces hostile currents which require iron determination.

The false façade each one presented during courtship has by this time started to crack, and disappointment necessarily must follow.

Have you ever heard the expression, "So-and-so died suddenly. The poor fellow wasn't even sick, just dropped dead."

What a short-sighted statement that is. No one ever dies suddenly, except in an accident. Sickness may be harbored within us for months, even years, without our having the slightest suspicion that we are actually dying all the time.

It is the same with love. One day you realize, with stark horror, that you have been living with a person who is repulsive to you. You can't understand for the life of you how you could ever have fallen in love with such an individual. It seems utterly fantastic that once upon a time you thought of him or her as the most "gorgeous and angelic" person who ever lived.

Is there a formula which can tell you when love starts to wither and will ultimately die? There's no such formula in existence, but there are telltale symptoms and very obvious little signs which foreshadow things to come. Here are a few:

Lack of appreciation	Lack of tenderness
Annoyance	Rudeness
Nagging	Belittling
Uncompromising attitude	Humiliation
Sarcasm	Stinginess
Regimentation	Being taken for granted
Indifference	Abuse
Fault-finding	Tardiness

There are many more indicative signs but we feel that the above are enough to remind you that what was once burning love began to be not so burning, then became tepid and finally downright cold.

These little, seemingly inconsequential symptoms are unnoticed, disguised first as very mild, polite annoyances. How is it possible for them to grow with such supersonic rapidity, almost overnight, into barbed-wire naggings and not only irritating but poisoned sarcasms? Can you guess what will happen next?

Look at the list. There you can see clearly the almost mathematical progression to hatred.

Let us take a young couple as an example, and see how great love can turn to hate.

These two young people fell madly in love. The girl was twenty-two and the boy twenty-five. They were sure that not even in history books could one find such undying love as theirs. It was heaven on earth. They defied their parents and eloped. Of course both of them were forced to work, although the girl had done nothing but attend college before she married. The boy was a clerk in an advertising firm. Evenings they were tired but happy. They enjoyed and loved every minute of their married life—at first.

On arriving home from work the boy would throw his clothes all over the place. It was sheer pleasure for him to do this because all his life he had had to be meticulously tidy. His mother was fanatical on this score.

There's a cruel but prophetic saying, "They were so much in love they had to marry to cool off." This "cooling off" came to pass quite early with our young married lovers.

After awhile the young wife became sick and tired of having to get up an hour earlier in the morning to pick up all the things her high-spirited spouse had scattered about. At first she was ashamed to mention this to him. He, on the other hand, was highly amused.

"This is fun, isn't it, honey?" he chuckled one morning as his little wife crawled under the bed to find his cuff link.

"It's not fun for me," she announced irritably.

This mild outburst was a real shocker to the young husband, so much so that he almost forgot to breathe. Then he sat down and whined piteously, "Don't make me feel married so soon! Don't ever use that tone with me again!"

"All right, I won't," she answered truculently, and crawled back into bed to doze for the rest of the precious minutes before she had to get up.

Being an inexperienced husband, he readily believed his wife's promise, and thought she would never use that accusing and irritated voice to him in the future.

She remained her same sweet self but started to insist, at first mildly and interspersed with beguiling kisses, that he should be more considerate and let her sleep in the morning, instead of asking her to find his wrist watch, his pocket comb, or his keys.

He began to realize slowly that something was amiss. He inquired quite acidly whether their honeymoon was over.

"What has my wanting to sleep a little longer in the morning got to do with our honeymoon?" she asked.

"Everything," he snapped at her. "If I can't have a wife who keeps a tidy house . . . we might as well call it quits!" he finished unreasonably.

"You mean divorce?" she asked breathlessly.

"I didn't say that."

"My hearing is absolutely normal. You said we should call it quits! What else does that mean if not divorce?"

"You'd better grow up, child."

"I'm not a child," she cried. "I'm a married woman!"

"Physically yes, but. . . ."

"Say it! Say it! I'm . . . I'm just. . . ."

"Just naive."

"I know something else is on your mind. You want a divorce, don't you?"

"I do not!" he shouted angrily. "What I meant, and I said it quite distinctly, was that we should call a halt to these nonsensical arguments."

"They're not nonsensical!" shouted the little woman. "I want to sleep and from now on don't you dare wake me up to find your stupid socks for you."

"Who's stupid?"

"I said your stupid socks!"

"Don't be a coward. Tell me you really meant to say that I'm stupid!"

"Okay, you're stupid," echoed the bride. "Are you happy now?"

That same night, however, their differences were overcome by their physical desire for each other.

A few months later they were invited to a party. The man, as usual, was ready and rarin' to go, but the dear little woman was still in the throes of those innumerable last-minute finishing touches which usually burn up the waiting male.

"Be a darling and find my white chiffon scarf for me," implored the young wife.

But her husband, still smarting from the rebuff two months earlier, remained seated and undisturbed.

"Did you find my scarf?" she asked a little later.

"No, my dear," he answered with the utmost calm. "I didn't."

"Didn't you look?"

"No, dear." His voice had a studied indifference.

"You didn't?" This was uttered in a high falsetto.

"No, dear. You told me not so long ago that I should look for my own things. You should do the same, dearest."

She gave him a venomous look and started to undress.

"Go to the party by yourself," she announced after a breathless silence. "I'm staying home."

"Are you sure, dear?" he asked politely.

"Positive."

"All right, then I'll be off. Good night, darling. Happy dreams. . . ."

And he really left.

When he came home he found the bird had flown. She was nowhere. No note, no wife. His first impulse was to burst out crying, because he really loved her. But somehow he remembered that he was supposed to be a man now, like his father. He had to be determined and strong.

He knew where she was—at her mother's, of course. And he was sure that she was waiting for his call, or for him to rush there to bring her back, begging for forgiveness. She could wait, he decided. He knew he must be determined so, with a heavy heart, he went to bed. He had nightmares. He was frightened out of his wits, but in the morning he was more determined than ever to resist the urge to phone or go for her.

With every passing hour he felt something heroic swelling within his chest. He had survived the first night and now he knew he would live through the second one. She would know in the future who was the head of the house.

By the fourth day he was miserable, wretched, and triumphant, all at the same time. He was on the verge of throwing in the sponge when his mother-in-law walked in unexpectedly.

She asked innocently, "Where's Annabelle?"

"With you, of course," he answered placidly. Now he knew that the hour of triumph had arrived. He felt drunk with power.

She conceded the fact, not by answering directly but by quite heatedly striking out in a different direction.

"You ought to be ashamed of yourself, letting that poor child eat her heart out. Have you no feelings? Go right to that phone and call her!"

"Why can't she call me?" he wanted to know.

"You're supposed to be a gentleman," she retorted acidly.

"That's true, and she's supposed to be a lady."

"You want her to come back, don't you?" she demanded.

"I didn't send her away," came the defiant answer.

Beginning to get very red in the face, she asked pointedly, "Do you want to end the marriage?"

"Ask her. I'll agree to whatever she wants."

"Even to divorce?" she asked incredulously.

"Whatever she wishes. If a divorce will make her happy, then I'll give her one."

"All right, but come and take her home first."

"No. I didn't send her away and I won't bring her back."

"You stubborn fool!" she cried, and charged out of the house.

Two hours later the door opened noiselessly and Annabelle came in. He pretended to read. Slowly she went into the bedroom and hung up her coat. She came back and looked at him, waiting for him to speak.

After an interval, as he was still immersed in his reading, she spoke first. "I'm home dear."

"That's nice," he said politely.

"Can I sit down?" she asked tremulously.

"Why, of course."

Annabelle sat down in his lap. "Do you mind?"

"Of course not." And suddenly the strength he had so heroically nurtured broke its bonds and he started to cry.

"For Heaven's sake, don't ever leave me!" he begged.

"I won't, darling," she promised, and they melted into a trembling, loving huddle.

And yet, ten years later, almost to the date of their wedding anniversary, they really did get a divorce.

What is behind this forbidding word "incompatibility?" Could people resolve their differences if they reasoned with each other? I think not. It often has nothing to do with understanding or reasonableness.

Let us look into one or two cases of incompatibility and see why the marriages were doomed to fail.

One young wife needed ten hours' sleep and stayed in bed until late in the morning, whereas her husband, a living dynamo, was wide awake after four or five hours' sleep. During the first year of their marriage it was fun to kid her about being a "sleeping beauty." But a couple of years later he became annoyed, then angry, then sarcastic, because in the late afternoon she was much livelier than he was. At night she was energetic, the life of the party, and at the ghostly hour of four in the morning was still going strong, as if she never intended to stop. They would go to bed, and he would be up at his usual hour, but she wouldn't stir until nearly noon. Finally he decided she was lazy. As a matter of fact, she was not. It was simply that her body required more sleep than his. However, his argument was that if she went to bed earlier, she would still have her ten hours' sleep but awaken at a reasonable hour in the morning, thoroughly refreshed.

She tried this but couldn't fall asleep until the wee hours of the morning, and when she got up she was only half-awake for ages. She struggled for months to break the habit until, exhausted, she was on the verge of a nervous breakdown. She loved her husband and desperately wanted to please him, but her body simply refused to respond to the requirements of this demanding man. Finally they arrived at the point of "incompatibility."

There are people who function best in the afternoon and evening hours, whereas others are at their best in the early hours of the day. When two such opposites marry they are, through no actual fault of either, incompatible.

This is only one facet of incompatibility. Another is the inability of some husbands and wives to play "follow the leader."

In society, equality is the most admirable concept by which to live, but in a partnership or marriage it will never work. You may dispute this statement if you like, but if you look around and see a happy partnership, friendship, or marriage, you will find that one of its members is the leader and the other the follower.

You are free to call this undemocratic behavior, unreasonable and degrading, nevertheless it is a necessity for harmonious co-existence. It is possible to have leadership without tyranny, as in the case of the brain, which first takes into account the physical condition of the body, then condenses and crystalizes the conflicting emotions, and upon arriving at a conclusion, gives the direction to move, to be outraged, to run from danger or fight back, depending upon the particular necessity of the moment.

When two people are dependent upon each other and their destination is the same, the leadership of one will not necessarily be ominous, nor will it compel dependency or slavery for the other.

Love is trust. Trust cannot be forced, it must be earned. Trust automatically places each person on the position of becoming a leader or a follower for the mutual benefit of both.

There is nothing degrading about this unconscious or conscious selectivity between two people which delegates one to leadership. They both can function for the benefit of each other if they know just what position they are going to fulfill in their future.

The trouble starts when two individuals with a virulent superiority complex are carried away by physical attraction and decide that they are madly in love.

In his book *What Is Science?* (Simon & Schuster) Erich Fromm states, "A man who is constantly bragging, boasting, belittling others, is perhaps aware of himself as a masterful superior person. What he's not aware of is that in reality all these feelings of power and superiority are only compensations for the very opposite. Deep down inside he feels weak, helpless, childish, and the very moment when he tells us, 'Look here, what a great guy I am,' he's really praying: 'Don't let them find out that I feel like a helpless child.' "

If both parties in a marriage happen to have the same compulsive superiority complex, each will fight tooth and nail to save it. Among such people compromise is impossible. Each will forever try to jockey for a better position to prove his mastery over the other. Incompatibility will be the result.

It is truly wonderful when young couples say and feel that

their love is the most sacred, the most genuine, in the history of man. The awakening of true love is the most thrilling experience in life.

Courtship is the time for a couple to get to know each other and find out how deeply each feels for the other. It is not an easy matter to detect meanness when it is covered with honey, but preliminary work must be done before one can trust or be trusted.

Lust and ignorance, for instance, are greatly responsible for people falling out of love.

Lust erupts like a volcano and dies out as quickly as it came. Real love is more controlled and, if it is cared for tenderly, can live and thrive for a lifetime. Tenderness is the touchstone of love. Of course, I don't mean to imply that love is just sunshine and honey. It requires tact, understanding and tolerance to smooth out the rough edges of living together. Two people can live with genuine love without bruising each other too much.

But when ignorance masquerades under the guise of love, it will erupt almost immediately and will be followed by recriminations, regret, and bitterness.

If a man shows signs of being frugal or, in plain English, stingy, during courtship, you can take it for granted that after marriage he'll be a holy terror where money is concerned.

Stinginess is really fear of tomorrow. To look ahead in order to avoid poverty is commendable foresight, but who can live with a person who is afraid twenty-four hours a day? Such a man stifles almost all manifestations of living. He knows only one virtue . . . to be safe. All other things are *verboten*.

If a frightened person happens to fall in love with one who is similarly attuned, there'll be a perfect unity between them.

But should a spendthrift happen to fall in love with a frugal person, their awakening will be horrible.

Frugal	—	Spendthrift
Healthy	—	Hypochondriac
Trusting	—	Liar
Honest	—	Dishonest
Vulgar	—	Refined
Conventional	—	Unconventional
Skeptic	—	Believer
Flirt	—	Retiring
Shiftless	—	Systematic
Oversexed	—	Undersexed
Materialistic	—	Spiritualistic
Sloppy	—	Meticulous
Moral	—	Immoral

etc.

There are countless more of such wrong combinations one must watch for, but let these few suffice for the time being. There are those, for instance, who have an absolute passion for music or sports or the theatre, and whereas the mate may really like any one of the above, he can't understand why his beloved should consider those things the very essence of life.

Now if one of the parties feels that the other is simply insane to be so madly in love with his own field of recreation and therefore starts a campaign or crusade to stop this great devotion, there will almost invariably be an obdurate and fanatical resistance.

Millions of couples stay together even after great disillusionment because of a sentimental and economic attachment to each other. But staying together and tolerating each other through force of habit is not love.

Let me define again what constitutes love: It is physical and mental attraction, plus emotional security.

Staying together when love is only a memory may be justified for the sake of convenience, or simply through a fear of loneliness. But why is it that a simple disillusionment can disturb people so much that many actually become ill over it? Why make such a fuss over such a small thing?

First of all, there is nothing small about being disillusioned. It means that our judgment was terribly wrong. We believed, we trusted, and we loved a person who turned out to be something other than that for which we had bargained.

To have trusted a person with your love—more, with your life—and to have the object of your admiration turn out to be something objectionable, evokes fear for your safety and your life.

Falling out of love is a major catastrophe, but fortunately it's very rarely fatal. Love is like the celebrated Phoenix: it will arise from its ashes and live again. With great caution we will start out to look once more for that one really great, redeeming, compensating emotion that makes living not only tolerable but a prolonged joy and ecstasy.

To love and be loved is the height of achievement. It is the greatest thing life has to offer.

It is the pinnacle of being important.

LOYALTY

There are many inspiring stories and plays hiding under the lofty concept of loyalty.

Here are a few.

Long, long ago a soldier was arrested for some kind of crime. The King thought he should be punished by death. The young soldier, who had been a brave and loyal subject, begged the King to be allowed to go back to his home before he was executed to say goodby to his elderly parents. He promised faithfully that he would be back in a week, in time for the execution.

The King laughed, saying he was not such a fool as to be taken in by such an empty promise, and the soldier was surely not such a fool as to come back to die.

But a friend of the condemned soldier stepped forward and said: "Your Majesty, I trust him. I will die in his stead if he breaks his promise."

Astonished by such blind trust the King answered, "I want you to know that if he fails to come back you will certainly die in his place!"

And the good friend said confidently, "I am not afraid. He'll be back, your Majesty."

The condemned soldier did come back, and the King was so impressed by the friend's sublime trust that he pardoned the soldier.

This is the kind of loyalty that poets like to write about.

Such loyalty need not be a fairy tale, either. It can exist when two or more people's interests so bind them together that life without the other seems impossible.

We must inspire loyalty.

And now here is a very strange kind of loyalty. Once upon a time there lived a couple so much in love that friends and even foes admitted that there was never such love on earth before.

By a strange misunderstanding, the young husband was arrested on a flagrant accusation that he was a spy for a foreign country. He was found guilty and it seemed that he would be executed in the shortest possible time. The young and beautiful wife was naturally overcome with grief, and as the execution neared she vowed that the same day her beloved husband died, she would follow him into eternity.

I have heard many strange stories about great love, when a man or a woman have declared that they could not survive the death of their beloved, and yet somehow managed to find someone who was ready to heal the wound and make them realize that after all, life is stronger than death, and they have managed quite happily to live to the end of their days.

There is always an exception to the normal. In this case, the soon-to-be bereaved woman meant what she had vowed. She knew that she would be loyal to her husband to her last breath.

But a very strange thing happened. The day before the execution, a very important personage representing the government appeared before the inconsolable young woman and told her that he had unquestionable evidence in his hands proving that her husband was innocent. And, to put it as bluntly as possible, he asked her if she were willing to entertain him for one single night in exchange for her beloved's life. He solemnly promised—nay, swore—that her husband would be free in a few days.

And now her loyalty came through with flying colors and proved to be 100 percent true till death. Clio, the immortal historian, has something to record for the ages. The young woman flatly refused the man's immoral proposition. She was ready to let her husband die rather than break her vow.

Then the unexpected happened. The very next day her husband was released. Of course there was joy, but only a Homer could have described the scene. The man was cleared completely, and they could have lived happily forever if the foolish woman, in a moment of exaltation, had not told him how her loyalty had been tempted but how nothing on earth could have induced her to be unfaithful to him.

The man's strong arms stiffened around her body, then pushed her away as he asked incredulously, "You refused to save my life?"

"I was loyal to you," she answered haltingly, frightened by the strange coolness in his voice.

The man was violent, and without a word. . . .

No, I won't finish this story either. I'll leave it to your imagination. As you see, there are loyalties and loyalties!

What is loyalty really—not in glittering words but in reality? Is it something that never changes? Is it anything that defies the erosion of time? The Sphinx and the pyramids, built to endure for eternity, are crumbling. A great metropolis, over whose streets swarm teeming millions, was once the bottom of an ocean, and in time to come will revert to an ocean bed which, in due time, will become a metropolis, and so on until this agonized earth explodes and is swallowed up in the fierce furnace of the sun.

"Everything is changeable—only change is eternal," goes the saying. It may be true that everything is changeable but loyalty. Isn't it indestructible? It must be, because if it is not, where can man pin his hopes for the future?

Shall we state the terrible truth that even loyalty is subject to the inexorable law of nature? We must say it because it is true! It changes as much as everything else.

Does it mean, then, that absolute loyalty never—but never —existed? Foolish question. It was and will be in existence as long as there are men who deserve it.

This attribute can live only in the warm and loving presence of another loyalty. Alone, it withers and dies of loneliness.

Where does one get more love and loyalty than from one's own parents? They actually are ready to give their lives that we should live.

Is that loyalty?

In a certain way it is.

It seems that we did not make a clear-cut definition. Let us start all over again. Loyalty should exist without any taint of selfishness or material gain. It should be as pure as the freshly-fallen snow. If we wished to emulate a sophist, we might well claim that no snowdrop could be pure because it is touched by the air—the atmosphere being full of miasma, germs, and filth.

No, there is no such thing as absolute purity in nature. Consequently, mother-love, too, must be more or less tainted by selfishness and self-interest.

It is still a noble feeling to love our offspring. We wish our son to succeed for his own and for our sakes. If he becomes an outcast, we would still help him, but deep down in our hearts we would be humiliated and ashamed that he failed us so miserably.

Why should parents expect anything from their offspring? It would be most unnatural if they didn't. If they did not believe and hope that their child would be special, they might not be so eager to produce one.

"My son, my son!" we dream . . . "He'll be the best of them all, of course." Since we always think that we are the focal point of the universe, naturally we think and believe that our offspring will be—should be—outstanding. Of course we have some sneaking doubts deep down in our hearts, and we pray: "Almighty God, if not outstanding . . . we are ready to settle for a healthy body and healthy mind," the two greatest gifts for which a parent can pray.

"My child." What sweetness is in those words. You are ready to protect him with your very life. And why not? This is not just any child. He's your very own, the continuation of yourself, past, present, and future. He is really you! The realization that through him you reach into the future, that you are being represented in successive generations perhaps to the end of time, this alone creates an emotion which surpasses even love. What you protect through your child is yourself. He is the epitome of life—your life. It is the highest goal for which to live. Why shouldn't one be loyal to one's self?

But life plays tricks, dirty tricks on us. Our beloved son is arrested for rape and murder. It is inconceivable! No, not our son! But our son confesses. There's no mistake about it. He's a murderer. But it can't be! There must have been brutality used against him to force him to confess. There was none. Our son says there was no brutality.

All right. Then he may be shielding someone. That's it! He's shielding someone. He's willing to die. Our son is willing to die for someone he loves. What heroism! What sacrifice! But he says that he isn't shielding anyone. What then? It is conclusively proven that he is guilty of first-degree murder of the most hideous sort.

What now?

Then he must be insane!. Of course. He is insane. (And we are sure, of course, that this didn't come from our side of the family!)

God Almighty! Help us!

Can you be loyal to an insane boy? You can't help it, for he still represents you, although your faith in the future is somewhat shaken. But do you still love this crimimal? Unfortunately, this criminal happens to be you. And being you, you would like to abandon him, but how in Heaven's name can you abandon yourself? So you stand behind him because, although you may hate yourself, you'll still try to salvage whatever you can from the wreckage.

If anyone thinks for even a moment that we are trying to be cynical about loyalty, he is mistaken. We bemoan our fate whenever loyalty, for whatever reason, goes on the rocks.

Usefulness gives birth to loyalty—but usefulness cannot be one-sided for long. The moment one realizes that the other party has stopped contributing his share, loyalty slowly shrivels up.

Does all this sound cold-blooded and calculated? It is merely factual. It is a natural process, like growing old.

Religion is something else again. Religion offers a helping

hand to those who believe, and even to those who stray and come back only when they are in need.

Religion also has its mortal enemy and fights desperately to remain alive. The Church offers faith in a better world after death to all those who believe and are loyal to her, and hell-fire for those who do not.

Loyalty in all strata of society acts for the same reason, that is, self-preservation. We do not think we have discovered a startlingly new concept when we point out that loyalty is a simple, reciprocal act in return for services rendered.

How about loyalty to our country? The country of our birth is usually the most sacred. We are born and intend to live and die there. Doesn't she deserve better treatment than a mere individual, organization, or even a church?

A country is like a fabulous mother, with millions of children. However, as long as one child is better off than another it is impossible to demand from all of them the same devotion. We can tell the poor, the neglected one, that he is obliged to be grateful just for the privilege of being alive. The poor and neglected one will not accept this as gospel truth, and in his bitterness might turn against us and even against his own mother when the pain, the neglect, the humiliation becomes unbearable.

We can preach to the hungry one till doomsday that turning against one's own mother or one's own country is the height of perfidy. Hungry people understand only one word: food! They will turn away from their mother or country without hesitation if someone else offers to fill their empty stomachs.

It is sheer madness to believe that a tortured man will keep his mother's or his country's name sacred because one brought him into this world and the other let him live to hunger without hope. Hungry people feel loyalty to no one.

The man who is robbed of the privilege of becoming im-

*portant in his own esteem or in the society in which he lives,
is a dangerous man. The importance of being important is
second only to self-preservation.*

HATE

R. A strange feeling came over me yesterday.

A. Tell me.

R. Something was gone from my life. Something very important.

A. What for instance?

R. Hate.

A. Do you mean to say you can't hate anymore?

R. Only God knows how I enjoyed hating an ex-friend of mine. . . . You see . . . once upon a time we were very close friends, schoolmates. I helped him in every way possible. I gave him money to go into business, and he became rich. He met his wife, a wonderful woman and a good mother, in my home. What else shall I tell you about him? I was not only a friend but also his adviser in all his financial matters, a father and mother rolled into one. In short, I was one of the family.

A. What happened to this beautiful friendship?

R. A poem.

A. I don't understand.

R. He wrote a poem.

A. What's wrong with that?

R. He never wrote a damn thing before. The fact is—he was not interested in literature, let alone poetry. He didn't give a hoot for books or for the theatre. His life was sports and nothing else.

A. Then he wrote a poem. And this one poem broke up a lifelong friendship?

R. Yes, it did, and I am convinced he did it on purpose. You see, I happened to be editor of a weekly literary

magazine. He arrogantly threw that stillborn idiocy
called a poem on my desk and demanded that I publish
it in the next issue. No preliminaries, no apologies, just
ordered me to take that thing without even reading it
first, and give it a prominent place in my magazine.
The audacity, the offhanded way of ordering me
around, made my blood boil. "What the devil do you
know about poetry?" I demanded after I had glanced
through his scatter-brained nonsense. "I know as much
as you do anytime!" he came back insolently, his voice
as sharp as a razor blade. The poem was not only atro-
cious, but it didn't even make sense.

A. Of course you were harsh with him.

R. What do you think?

A. Then you started a fight.

R. He asked for it, so I gave it to him—good.

A. You felt insulted?

R. Of course I felt insulted. That illiterate moron dared
to ask me to put such nonsense into my paper.

A. Have you found out why he acted as he did? No doubt
there was a provocation. The question is, why?

R. Yes, I thought a great deal about it—I hated his guts—
until yesterday.

A. What happened yesterday?

R. Suddenly I saw the whole picture. I, the benefactor, the
wise, the generous man, had been walking in and out of
his life like an infallible demi-god. I remembered
rudely interrupting him in the middle of a sentence
like an intolerant grouchy old father who will not stand
for the slightest contradiction from his son. I remembered seeing him flush with anger at things I said and
his wife gently nudging him so he wouldn't oppose me.
And that poor guy had tolerated me in his home for,

let me see, twelve or thirteen years. His tolerance and humility would have been a shining example to Job.

A. And now you've stopped hating him?

R. Let me put it this way. With the persistence of a fanatic, you've been hammering home the point that all of us, out of sheer necessity, build a front for ourselves. I had enjoyed hating that moron so long—when suddenly it hit me. "Gosh, that poor sap would have been justified in kicking me the hell out of his house. After all, he's entitled to be king in his own home." I decided to stop hating him, but hate is like a nice plaything—hard to give up.

A. But if you know that your friend was more than justified in provoking you....

R. I'm sure you know the answer.

A. Perhaps, but I'd like to hear whether you know it.

R. I was proven wrong and, as you know, we never like to be caught in the wrong. All right, my mistake was in being overbearing and boorish—but I am sure there was plenty of reason for it. He made plenty of mistakes and like a good father-protector, I was on the job. . . .

A. Now you are rationalizing.

R. Why should I take all the blame? I am absolutely convinced that if I hadn't stopped him in many of his crazy investment schemes, he would have lost his shirt.

A. Do you believe all this?

R. Not necessarily. I try to do only what everyone would in my place, minimize my mistakes and prove that the other fellow deserved what he got. Period. I know, don't tell me . . . my front again. . . . My lousy importance has to be kept intact at least before myself, even if I lose face before the world.

A. The question is whether you hate him or not.

R. I see his point now and I wonder if he can see mine.

A. What is your point?

R. That I make him see that I only wanted to help him. He should understand that my role of a protecting father sprang from his accepting the money from me to start his business.

A. That's true, but it's also true you constantly reminded him that he was in your debt and would remain there until you are dead. What a cruel prospect! You actually refused to let him grow up, or think for himself, until his resentment became a cancerous growth and he decided to cut you out of his life, whatever the cost might be.

R. Yes, yes, it must have happened that way.

A. Since he waited so long to get rid of you, it shows that his affection towards you was real. I believe that he loved you and tried to please you, but you stubbornly refused to let him alone. You wanted to choke all initiative in him to death. Is that right?

R. Of course not. Now look, let's stop this nonsense. I told you I've stopped hating him. But I can't help rationalizing and justifying myself.

A. I see that. Rationalizing is our last line of defense. How about your two sons? Why did they leave you? Would you care to tell me?

R. It's hard to admit that one is wrong, but the rationalization of what actually happened between me and this ex-friend of mine tore away the subterfuge of self-delusion and I can't blame the other fellow any longer.

A. What are you trying to say?

R. That I was an overbearing father to them too. They hate my guts. I wanted them to come into my business but they had different ideas. The fact is, as I see it now, they just wanted to go away from me as far as possible.

A. You are a modern man, you should have known. . . .

R. Yes, I should have—but I didn't. I see now that every
living man starts early to build himself a world of his
own. He wants to be the king of his world and resents
anyone daring to step into this secret territory. No tres-
passing is allowed.

A. Yes, this is true.

R. He may have all the degrees a college can bestow, but
he is still liable to forget that everyone has as big a dose
of ego and self-respect as the next fellow, and will never
tolerate any belittling or benevolent attitude toward
him. We may as well learn that we had better talk to
every individual not as an inferior but as an equal.

Now at last it has penetrated into my thick skull
that my sons left me because I looked upon them as my
private property and not as individuals.

The strangest phenomenon, it seems to me now, is the
awareness that in all strata of society there is nothing greater
in a man's life than *The Importance of Being Important.*

11

X-Raying a Character

I intend to explore heredity in this chapter. No writer can afford to overlook this vital element of the character he writes about. It is not always lovelessness or poverty which motivates cruelty and intolerance. Inherited characteristics must take an important part of the blame.

Unfortunately, most of us attach too much importance to environment, and often overlook the inherited characteristics which have such an important role in the shaping of human destiny.

For this reason I wish to discuss people who refuse to move, to change, to be convinced, and to understand the obvious.

Everyone brings into this world the blessings or curse of his ancestors. Leonardo da Vinci, the greatest genius who ever lived, owed a great deal to his progenitors. So did Adolf Eichmann, Himmler, Hitler.

Dr. Lester R. Aronson, head of the Department of Animal Behavior of the American Museum of National History, states that so far as behavior is concerned, "Heredity is 100 percent important and environment is also 100 percent important."

We cannot get away from the fact that our physical make-up will influence our future personality. If we happen to be deficient in even only one of the elements necessary for proper functioning, it will show up sharply and we shall be sick. Let us suppose that we do not get enough calcium, which comes from dairy products and fruit; our bone structure will be porous and the smallest fall will result in the breaking of some bone. If we happen to lack iron, we will slowly but surely become anemic.

In short, health is the fundamental factor of our future and the future of our children. We intend to see what happens to children who are born with chemical deficiencies—how they act and react to normal everyday stimuli.

Dr. Howard Fabing, Cincinnati neuropsychiatrist, and many other psychiatrists and scientists have come to the conclusion that biological causes start destructive mental illness on its way.

The August, 1958, issue of *Archives of Neurology and Psychiatry,* published by the American Medical Association, came out with really startling evidence that the most baffling form of mental disease, schizophrenia, is caused by a brain deficiency.

No one needs to be a doctor to know that an upset stomach can make one dizzy; chronic constipation causes acute autointoxication. Wrong diet may cause low or high blood pressure or diabetes or make the bloodstream sluggish; in consequence the brain function slows down and thinking becomes painful. In such a state we do things which otherwise we would consider outright idiotic.

It was found that hypersensitiveness, bad metabolism, lack of initiative, and lack of capacity to make decisions are the direct result of a thyroid dwarfed by malnutrition, while overactivity of the same gland causes anxiety and fear.

The right food, then, for expectant mothers makes the difference between life or death—not to mention the fact that if a defective child survives, its personality will be directly affected.

Right now we don't know specifically what an habitual criminal lacks in the chemical laboratory of his body. But we are sure that the unbalanced diet of his prospective mother at the time of his conception (even long before his conception), coupled with an unfortunate environment, make him retarded or incapable of obeying law and order.

Habitual criminals are retarded people. Their activity outside the law proves that. They do not have the foresight to realize that they cannot win against the law. They do not know that they have no chance to win against scientific detection.

Retarded people are born, not made. Anyone who does wrong constantly, not for the purpose of spiting anyone, although it may quite often seem so, must be sick first and criminal second. Such people in reality can't help themselves.

We can and do put them in prison for their criminal activities over and over again until they die. But that does not help them. Nor does society gain by their imprisonment. These people are sick. They'll soon be back in prison if we let them out. Some of them commit crime after crime like clockwork, because that's the only way they can express themselves.

V. H. Mottram, Professor of Psychology at Kings College of the University of London, states in *The Physical Basis of Personality,* "Our personality depends on our physical bodies and on the genes we inherit. We are what we inherit and that is determined to the last hair on our eyebrows or the freckles on our skin."

Youthful delinquency, like unhappy marriages, must be corrected not through courts or prisons but through love and rebuilding the chemical make-up of retarded and deficient bodies.

Here is a most revolting but at the same time revealing murder that happened in Chicago on March 16, 1957. Twelve teenagers, all from "decent" families, decided to kill someone and—but let them tell it themselves, as all of the metropolitan newspapers reported it:

"Two cars were ready to start out. Someone said, 'What are we going to do?' Someone else said, 'Let's go out and get a nigger.'

"Another somebody said, 'I need some money.' Somebody else said, 'I need a topcoat.' I said I needed shoes.

"Ray said, 'I'll hit him first. I'll bring him down and take his money and you guys can take what you want.'

"I said, 'I'll take his shoes. And another kid said, 'I'll take his jacket.'"

Schwartz, who said he was tanked up with beer and wine, got out of the car when they stopped for a traffic light at 59th and Kedzie Streets, where they spotted Palmer, a slight young Negro, waiting for a bus.

Schwartz approached his victim. A witness said he used both hands to swing the hammer. One of the rebels yelled "Let's get out of here."

Everybody ran. Everybody, that is, but Schwartz, who swung at another Negro standing there and grazed his shoulder before he fled.

It was all as senseless and cruel as the murders committed by the four Brooklyn "thrill killers," fifteen to eighteen, who were convicted in 1955 of torturing and drowning a factory worker. Their idea of sport was to go into a park near the East River and torture and beat vagrants and drunks. They set one man on fire with gasoline and were accused of burning the feet of others and beating a steeplejack to death.

"At the time I didn't think I was doing anything bad," Melvin Mittman, seventeen, the strong-arm man of that gang, wrote after his conviction.

Although Joseph Schwartz did not explain the hatred that was in him when he swung the hammer at a youth he had never seen before, it was obvious at the inquest that he was

filled with resentment against his father. As the older
Schwartz was testifying, the boy glared at him.

The father said his wife had been in a mental institution
and he had tried to be both father and mother to their two
children. He said Joseph had walked out some time before,
having quarreled when he was asked to contribute something
toward his board. He thought Joseph was living with his
elder brother, William Jr., had a job in the railroad yards,
and was not in need.

A portly, red-faced man, he said he had no idea that his son
had any hatred for Negroes. "Why, I'm a milkman and many
of my customers are Negroes," he said. "Now what will they
think about me? This is a terrible thing."

Mrs. Anna Bandyk, mother of Jerome, one of the accused
boys, said (as did most of the parents) that her son was a
"good boy" who didn't drink or carry weapons and had never
before been in trouble.

"My husband is very strict with our four boys," she said.
"They have good clothes to wear and plenty to eat, and go to
church. It's just beyond me."

Police Lieutenant Michael Delaney, head of the Juvenile
Bureau, apparently knew the boys' potentiality for evil better
than the parents did. He knew the Rebels had been operat-
ing for two years, were organized into junior and senior divi-
sions, and lived by the code of the street gangs, to whom all
outsiders are enemies.

You will notice that all the parents claimed that their sons
were "good boys." No doubt they might have been good,
polite, and at times generous to an unfortunate. Most of these
good boys lived with loving parents. What could have happened to them? Had these youthful murderers *suddenly* gone
berserk?

Anyone who cannot visualize the outcome of a misdeed
must be mentally deficient, whether he is a good boy or not.

Our six-year-old son confronted us one day during the First World War and declared that he was ready to go to the battle-field and kill all the enemy. After making this heroic and historic declaration, he waited for some kind of reassurance from us.

Without any hesitation we gave our permission to end the war by single-handedly exterminating all the dastardly enemies. Only we warned our determined son what might happen to him should the enemy, who through some oversight also had guns and bombs and tanks, shoot a few unfriendly bullets into him.

He didn't like the prospect at all, and asked dubiously, "Will they be allowed to kill me?"

"Yes, dear," we assured him. "They have the same right to kill as you."

After a moment we asked our vacillating and deeply disturbed son, "Are you still ready to go to war?"

He dismissed the whole affair with an emphatic "Whew!" —whatever that meant.

We are absolutely sure that those four youthful killers must have heard on the radio, must have seen on TV, that crime and brutality do not pay. They must have heard all this from their parents and in school and in their church. It obviously did not penetrate their minds as it did our six-year-old son's. They didn't have the mental capacity to absorb an obvious truth. It is obvious, we say, because they were old enough by then to know that society cannot tolerate barbarism if it wishes to survive.

We doubt if there is one sane human being who has not thought once in a while of committing something unlawful, even destructive. But most of us refrain from going through with it because we not only can reason out but actually visualize the dire results of our calculated and planned misdeed.

Anyone who cannot draw a conclusion is deficient mentally! Such people, be they young or old, should be examined for physical and nutritional deficiencies and get help in rebuilding the faulty chemical structures of their bodies.

We have seen with our own eyes just such miraculous transformations.

Yes, there is hope for those who desire to live with their fellow men in peace.

The differences between a moronic and an intelligent person are many. The normal, intelligent person is one who has the ability to learn.

A moronic person is not necessarily abnormal in any sense of the word. He can work and accomplish manual tasks he has learned, but his I.Q. of 75 is still that of a child of seven to ten. Such a man can go through life like anybody else without much difficulty—*if he is left alone*. He can do simple manual or intelletual labor of a routine sort, but if any complication arises he will be hopelessly lost. He has no inventiveness, no resources with which to create new ideas.

Such people cannot change because they cannot conceive of any other way to do a job than the one to which they were accustomed in the past. Anyone who cannot change, even though the change is imperative for his own survival, must be mentally defective. The inherited characteristics must be fatal when *two* mentally defective people bring forth a child. It comes into the world with an overgrown albatross around its neck.

With the mentally-retarded individual, anger is usually impotent rage. Ex-convict G.R., twenty-three, was arrested for raping three women. He had been in trouble before for stealing and assault. Whenever he gets out after he has paid his debt to society, he'll be back in prison in short order.

John Francis Roche was executed on August 26, 1955, for the rape and murder of a fourteen-year-old girl. He admitted five other murders.

Sometimes in one day there are three or four such items in the daily papers. Criminals without conscience or foresight are the products not only of bad environment but inherited characteristics to boot, although they might have been a genius I.Q.

Let a man be even at the lowest point of human intelligence; the desire *to be noticed, to show off, to be important,* burns as fiercely in him as in a normal person—if not more fiercely. It must be stronger in him because there's no restraining reasoning power to hold him back or to point a warning finger at the danger awaiting him if he steps into the forbidden territory of the outlaw.

The mental reasoning of such a person is muffled, and the overpowering desire to succeed, to be important, to be admired by his fellow defectives—and himself—rules out all caution.

And what a pity to know that a few common elements—at the time of conception—could have made them as normal as the best of men.

A writer can't help but profit by knowing the source, the motivation, of why his character acts the way he does. Every act is not necessarily the result of a whim or a caprice but the logical—or unlogical—conclusion of the particular chemical make-up of our system.

"Genius is the happy result of a combination of many circumstances," says Havelock Ellis in his book, *The Study of British Genius.* I agree with Ellis. Our inherited characteristics are precisely what make possible the happy result Ellis is talking about. The happy result is one of the gifts we have received from our cursed or blessed progenitors; the other is the stimulating and healthy environment in which a child can grow to maturity.

Bravado, a death-defying stunt, even a murder could be a superb substitute for importance. Man consciously, more often than not subconsciously, would commit a hair-raising act just to impress his fellow men.

In Conclusion

Let me remind you, if you happen to see a play of antiquity, or read a book which survived generations, you can't fail to realize that only strong, unbending, ruthless characters —whether they served heaven or hell—could survive and live through the vicissitude of changing times and remain fresh or new.

There never was and never will be a more exciting theme or story than the revelation of a three-dimensional character.

I devoutly hope that this book will help you to realize your ambition to be not only a successful writer—but an enduring one.

Good Luck to You.

APPENDIX I

The Basic Principles of Writing

It is imperative that every type of writing should contain the following:

> Premise
> Pivotal character or characters
> Character (three-dimensional)
> Unity of opposites
> Growth
> Orchestration
> Point of attack
> Conflict
> Transition
> Crisis
> Climax
> Resolution

These twelve parts are as indispensable in writing as are the vital organs to the human body.

PREMISE

The premise is the seed from which the story grows. The premise is the thumbnail synopsis of the story or play you wish to write.

It isn't compulsory, but it is wise to formulate your premise first. You might have an idea or have read or heard something that seems to constitute a good story idea. No matter where your inspiration comes from, you must know exactly what you want to say, why you want to say it, and how far you want to carry it.

If your story pertains to greed, to which you are opposed, you'll want to know in what direction and how far you intend to go with this idea, what will be its final resolution. This crystalization of your story is the premise.

You might want to say: "Greed leads to destruction," or "Greed leads to humiliation," or "Greed leads to isolation," or "Greed leads to loss of love." You can go on indefinitely, formulating premises for yourself, but when you decide on *one,* capture the one which expresses *your* idea perfectly. Then you have your story in a nutshell.

The premise should include the basic facts about the *character, conflict,* and *resolution.* For instance, "Honesty is the best policy" is not the best premise. We see the character, an honest person. But where is the conflict? This person is honest all through life and all through the play; he's very happy, nobody bothers him. A wonderful life—but a very bad play. But—if we use the premise, "Honesty defeats duplicity"— we know immediately that our honest person is going to engage in conflict with a dishonest person. There is inherent drama in this premise.

In short, the first part of any premise should represent character: honesty, dishonesty, selfishness, ruthlessness, false pride, etc. The second part should represent conflict: "Dishonesty leads to exposure," "Ruthless ambition leads to destruction," etc. The third part should represent the resolution or goal of the play or story.

As we see, a good premise is an indispensable part of good writing. A premise is a goal.

Many so-called scholars ridicule the idea of working out a premise before starting to write a play or story. They state that great stories were written before anyone knew anything about premises. This is true. But it is also true that even the greatest writers wrote more bad plays or stories than good ones. Without direction (a premise), they floundered!

When one intends to drive a car from New York to San Francisco, he usually uses a road map for more direct routes and good roads. The premise is the road map for all kinds of writing.

The next thing we ask is, who is going to carry out the author's premise . . . the characters?

Let's see if this is true. Let us suppose that we are intrigued by a braggart. We want to write about him. He claims that he comes from excellent stock, knows the best people, knows everything, in fact. He earns a lot of money, has the greatest hope for the future, and, according to him, he's the greatest guy he knows.

Naturally not a word of this is true. You're justified in asking, "Why all the bluff? The answer is, the poor fellow really has nothing whatsoever to boast about, so he concocts these grand and glorious lies. Bluffers, liars, boasters usually do this sort of thing to cover up their physical or mental inadequacies.

Now, how can this story end? Failure and humiliation for this character seem obvious. So if you're going to write a story about such a character, don't you think it is wise to know in advance how he's going to end up?

If you know the end of your story before you start to write it, you are in a better position to write a good one. Find out who your character is, where he comes from, why he is a failure. Because it's his failure he's trying to cover up with his lying. If you have this advance knowledge, you are in a better position to do a more thorough job.

For such a story I think the premise should be: "Bragging leads to humiliation." This play or story can be a drama, satire, or both, but never a comedy. However, you can make a fine comedy out of the bragging idea if you change your premise to read like this: "Bragging leads to success." Read *The Show-Off* by George Kelly. It is a satirical comedy written on the above premise.

You'll do better if you try to crystalize whatever you want to say and find your premise before you begin to write.

PIVOTAL CHARACTER

Now, who is going to force the characters into action? The honest person may never be troubled by his dishonest friend (to quote our first premise) unless one of the characters forces the issue and in so doing creates conflict. This person would be called the pivotal character. The pivotal character forces the conflict from beginning to end in play, story, or novel. The other characters may be uncertain as to what they want or where they want to go, but the pivotal character knows immediately what he wants.

A selfish person is selfish when the play opens. He is *relentlessly selfish*. The pivotal character is always relentless. A pivotal character is not motivated by a whim. He has a duty to perform. He must force the conflict to the bitter end, never backing down in the middle of the play or story.

He is relentless because circumstances beyond his control force him to be relentless. If an honest man steals, it is not for the thrill or luxury of it. It is because his family is starving, or perhaps because there is illness. This pressing need for money is a matter of life or death. A man can murder because of a ruthless ambition, desire for revenge, frustration, etc. But whatever the reason, it must be a relentless one.

When the pivotal character stops forcing the conflict, the story ceases too.

The pivotal character usually wishes change. He's dissatisfied. He is militant, ruthlessly militant, whether fighting for or against his status quo.

The pivotal character is the motivating power; he's the cause of conflict in your story or play. If he's ambitious, he won't hesitate to commit blackmail. He must be cunning and ruthless and, if necessary, ready to commit murder in order to achieve his goal, whether his goal is for good or for evil. If he's a good pivotal character, he holds nothing sacred and feels that nothing can stop him from reaching his goal.

If a writer doesn't understand the mechanism of a pivotal character, he won't know in what direction his story is going. The pivotal character knows where he's going, and tries to force everyone to go his way. If the antagonist refuses to go along with him, it's not because the pivotal character didn't push him hard enough. The pivotal character is a stubborn individual who sees only his own goal.

The pivotal character is the heart of all stories, pumping in all the conflict. If he stops pumping, your story or play stops living, just as your body would stop living if the bloodstream were cut off.

I wonder if you can define the difference between a conservative and a reactionary?

The conservative is satisfied with himself, his country, and the world as they are, and wishes to keep them that way; but he's too busy or too lazy to fight for this principle. He feels that everything will come all right in the end.

The reactionary, on the other hand, wishes to keep his life and everything else as is, like the conservative, except that he will go all-out to fight for his principle, and, if necessary, will die for it.

The difference between a liberal and a radical is the same. The former feels that the world needs a change, but hopes that somehow things will work themselves out in the long run.

The radical, however, instead of wishing or waiting, goes all-out and fights for what he sincerely believes in.

The pivotal character is always on the side of the militant. He is militancy personified. Only great passion makes pivotal characters.

Here are a few examples of pivotal characters:

He wants to take *revenge* on the man who ran away with his wife.

He wants to take *revenge* on the man who sent him to prison on a trumped-up charge and took his business away.

He wants to take *revenge* on the man who ruined his daughter and refused to marry her.

He *loves* a woman madly but he must make money first to marry her.

He is willing to *give his life* for his country, which he loves more than anything in this world.

He is willing to *be a martyr* for his religious belief.

He is *greedy*. His greediness sprang from poverty, and now he ruthlessly exploits others for fear of hunger.

He is ready to *destroy* others to achieve his goal.

He may *want* to be a musician or a scientist or a dancer or an inventor, etc.

Great men are usually outstanding pivotal characters; great criminals also belong in the same category.

CHARACTER

The third important factor in writing a story is to look for "character." Who are these people? Where do they come from? What was their childhood like? What is their background? What are their plans in life, their dreams, hopes, ambitions, frustrations, and complexes?

Character is the vital material with which an author must work. Thus, he must know this subject thoroughly.

Every object has three dimensions: depth, height, and width.

Human beings have three additional dimensions: physiology, sociology, and psychology.

It is not enough to know that a man is rude, polite, religious, atheistic, moral, or degenerate. We must know why. Why is he any of these things? Why is his character constantly changing, and why must it change whether he wants it to or not?

The first dimension, the physical, covers the appearance and general health of the character. A healthy person reacts differently to things from an unhealthy one. Health makes the difference in his attitude toward life. It may make him tolerant or humble, defiant or arrogant. It affects his mental development, resulting in either an inferiority or a superiority complex.

The general idea that beautiful women are dumb has its foundation in the fact that life has been made easier for them. People are supposed to cater more to beautiful individuals, men or women, which means that they have to exert less ingenuity to attain any object in their favor. A less attractive woman has to work hard for her achievement or accomplishment, which in turn sharpens her mind and molds her into a better person.

The sociology of the character is the second dimension. There is a vast and obvious difference between children born in slums and those born in the lap of luxury.

Environment means home life, marital status of parents, earning power, whether divorced, widowed, compatible, or incompatible. How did the character's friends affect him and how did he affect them. What schooling did he have? What was his attitude in school, his favorite subjects, his special aptitudes? What kind of social life did he lead?

The third dimension, the psychological, is the result of the previous two dimensions. This third dimension will give life to ambitions, frustrations, temperaments, attitudes, and complexes of the character.

To understand the actions of an individual we must first find his motivation.

Does a man have large ears, bulging eyes, long, hairy arms? Does he dislike talking about crooked noses, large mouths, thick lips, large feet? Perhaps he does, because he has one of these defects. One person may resign himself to physical handicaps, another pokes fun at them, while a third may be resentful. Many people do not escape the effects of a particular shortcoming. You must know your characters even better than you know yourself.

UNITY OF OPPOSITES

In a good play each character must serve a purpose. He should be an integral part of the whole structure so that if he is removed, the structure collapses.

How can the author integrate each and every character he selects? Simply by creating a bond between the characters or what is known as a unity of opposites. These people might oppose one another, but they cannot walk out on each other because they are united by a common bond. However, when certain character traits are broken or changed, there is an out.

A wife hates her husband. Why doesn't she divorce him? First, because they have children; second, she is dependent upon him financially. Usually children alone cannot bind the characters together, except when there is an extraordinary love for them. There must be something greater at stake. For instance, money, business, honor, revenge, threatened murder, blackmail, etc.

For our unity of opposites we ask this question: What is the unbreakable bond between the characters? What is so much at stake that they cannot leave each other?

In Hemingway's "The Killers," the unrelenting search for the man they are to kill constitutes the unbreakable bond.

In Maupassant's "The Necklace," vanity is an excellent unity of opposites.

In Jack London's "Making a Fire," the unbreakable bond is the freezing cold against the man's hopeless struggle to live.

In Betty Smith's *A Tree Grows in Brooklyn,* the mother's unselfish devotion to her children constitutes the necessary bond.

In *Hamlet* it was revenge for the father's death.

In *Othello* it was Iago's determination to revenge himself on Othello.

In *A Doll's House* it was Nora's love for her children and her financial dependency upon her husband. (In Ibsen's time women did not work.)

In *Romeo and Juliet* it was the title characters' deathless love for each other.

Love, ordinary love, cannot be a good unity of opposites. The love must be great, deep, and death-defying if it is to serve as a strong enough bond. Let us assume the premise of a story to be, "Possessive love leads to isolation." The pivotal character would be the selfish person. Let's make her a mother who, under pretense of sacrifice, tries to ruin her children's lives. She tries to separate them from their spouses because she's jealous of them. She demands her children's constant attention. Her children are bound to her because of loyalty, love, pity (she might be ill or financially dependent upon them), or because they are in the habit of obeying her every whim.

Breaking the bond would come when the children's love has turned to disgust, disillusionment, and loss of loyalty. They would finally see through their self-sacrificing mother and leave her all alone, stranded. This is the premise of *The Silver Cord.*

GROWTH

Everyone needs nourishment in order to grow. In order to have growth in writing, we must feed it with conflict. Conflict results from contradiction. Contradiction is the outgrowth of two strong wills, desperately straining against each other. Desperation is an empty phrase unless we understand that it springs from hopelessness.

Frustration grows from disappointment. A tiny bit of frustration might grow into tragedy.

Again, conflict is contradiction. Contradiction, animosity, fear, jealousy, covetousness, hate, and ruthless ambition: these are the ingredients upon which conflict thrives. Just as a person cannot live without sustenance, conflict cannot grow and thrive without our feeding it with troubles and miseries.

It is the duty of the writer to feed these human passions generously, if he would later have them work for him.

In attempting to rectify one wrong decision we commit another, then commit a third to rectify the second, ad infinitum. Some persons will concede defeat in time to prevent destruction. Others who are stubborn and tenacious will never give up. They'll defy pressing circumstances. They'll carry on against all the laws of organized society.

So, for the express purpose of drama, a writer should be interested only in characters who, by their physical and environmental make-up, are predestined to attempt to cut through life like the ancient who cut the Gordian knot with a sword. These characters are reckless people. They burn with a holy zeal. They try to achieve their goal, no matter what the price. However, these ruthless people become desperate *only after dire necessity* forces them to a decision and any delay in acting might cost them their lives, wealth, health, or honor. Desperate necessity propels these characters toward their ultimate goal, clearly stated in the original premise. Thus, every living character grows only through conflict.

Persons grow and change every second of their lives. Some people grow rapidly, others more slowly. Husbands and wives living together for years may change so gradually it will hardly be noticeable to themselves. But a person who has not seen them for years will be startled by the perceptible changes.

Drama is not life itself, but the essence of life. Within the space of two hours' time, we must see tremendous growth in characters. The greater the conflict in human life, the faster and more apparent the growth. Since on the stage a lifetime must be condensed into two hours, the changes must be great.

In a novel, the growth is more measured. The author can take his time. He can follow his characters through the years to the end of their days. However, the characters must still grow. For instance, a selfish person might grow to be generous, a jealous person become trusting, a loyal person turn disloyal. This pole-to-pole growth and how it happens makes the most exciting story in any form.

Orchestration

It is a truism that everything has its opposite. There is no light without a shadow; life is a contradiction to death. Opposition or contradiction exist even in the stars, where an invisible adhesive power called gravitation prevents our pitifully small earth from being smashed into pieces. The same laws govern the invisible atom, where the positron exerts the unifying force amid the positive and negative electrons and protons, while they pull and push each other around like mad dervishes.

Contradiction, the basic principle of life, is manifest also in the creation of the arts. The compositions of the dance are unthinkable without contradiction in movement. The same holds true in painting, where opposing lines and colors create a desired unity. In music, harmony cannot exist without dis-harmony.

The same law governs all writing. Contradictory characters pitted against one another, such as naive against worldly-wise, evil against just, clash while the all-powerful premise, the equivalent of the positron in the atom, will be the unifying force which will drive the contradictory characters toward their predestined ends. When contradictory characters are unified by the premise, we have orchestration.

Without good orchestration, no intelligent composition is possible. We have to be alert and find contradictions every-where. If we fail to find them, it will not be because they do not exist, but because we failed.

Is there such a thing as injustice? Yes, there is. If you do something against me, that act is unjust. If I do something against you, that act is just. Apparently a third force must exist like the positron and the sun in this case, a judge, to coordinate this seemingly unharmonious contradiction.

If there weren't any force to control these contradictions, life would not be possible.

Let us say once again that contradiction is everywhere and in all of us. Nora in *A Doll's House* is naive, her husband Helmer is worldly-wise.

All good plays, novels, and short stories are based on the same principles:

Honesty	—Dishonesty
Conventionality	—Unconventionality
Morality	—Immorality
Generosity	—Miserliness
Impracticability	—Reality
Superstition	—Science
Trustfulness	—Distrustfulness
Scrupulousness	—Unscrupulousness
Responsibility	—Irresponsibility

Now imagine these opposites in conflict!

Taking for granted that these people are *militant* in their beliefs and bound together by an unbreakable bond, what uproarious comedy or stark tragedy can be produced!

POINT OF ATTACK

Some plays, novels, even short stories are so slow in starting that they seem as if they will never lead anywhere. We find ourselves so bored that we are ready to toss away the novel or leave the theatre.

The point of attack should start your story. A story and especially a play must open with a crisis which is the sole point of attack—in the life or lives of one or more of the characters. A decision must be imminent and the characters must be ready to take action.

A married couple may quarrel bitterly for twenty years. They may threaten to leave each other. The question is: At what point in the lives of this couple would the author start his play? The answer is: When one of them is about to make a decision, or when the point of crisis is reached. Many things may have occurred between these people before we meet them. We are only interested in meeting them when they have reached a crisis in their lives and are about to take a decisive step.

Every short story, novel, and play should start in the middle of the middle. Read *The Killers* by Hemingway, or the play *Born Yesterday* by Garson Kanin. If you wish to write a good short story or novel, start on the note of crisis.

No law states that you cannot start your story in any other way. But if you want to catch the reader's interest *immediately*, you had better start with a conflict.

CONFLICT

Even people who know little about the mechanics of writing are bored by a static play, a play which has little conflict or spotty conflict.

There are four types of conflict: foreshadowing, static, jumping, and slowly rising.

Foreshadowing conflict should appear at the beginning of the play. Crisis is the hint or the promise of future conflict. In the motion picture *Thirty Seconds Over Tokyo,* almost the entire picture consisted of foreshadowing conflict. The soldiers were training for a mission so dangerous that utmost secrecy was necessary. They weren't even allowed to discuss the mission among themselves. The soldiers' training, that could have been monotonous to watch, proved enrapturing to the audience because of the foreshadowing of the life-or-death mission planted in the very beginning.

In *Romeo and Juliet* the families were such bitter enemies that even the servants of the respective households were ready to kill each other on sight. What chance did the young lovers have?

When Nora in *A Doll's House* naively thinks her husband Helmer will be grateful that she forged her father's signature to save his life, we wait for him to find out, knowing that Helmer is the epitome of honesty—and can never forgive.

Future events, future conflicts, must be foreshadowed at the beginning.

In static conflict the conflict remains on an even keel, rising only momentarily. Since life constantly changes and nothing in life is ever static, static conflict is found only in bad writing.

Arguments and quarrels create static conflict, unless the characters are growing and changing during the arguments. Every movement, every line of dialogue must further the action toward the final goal.

In jumping conflict the characters jump from one emotional plane to another, eliminating the necessary transitional steps.

Nature never jumps. A seed planted in the soil one day does not produce a flower the next. During the interval many transitions take place before the plant finally blooms. In the play, the author plants the seeds of his characters' growth, and slowly, step by step, they grow, the changes being witnessed by the spectators.

Static and jumping are the two deadly mistakes of all writing. They must be avoided at all cost.

If you wish to avoid jumping or static conflict you must know in advance what road your characters must travel, for instance:

> Drunkenness to sobriety
> Sobriety to drunkenness
> Timidity to brazenness
> Brazenness to timidity
> Simplicity to pretentiousness
> Pretentiousness to simplicity
> Fidelity to infidelity

The above represent two poles, the first the starting point, the second the arrival point. If you master this simple rule you'll have rising conflict throughout your story or play.

TRANSITION

Let us suppose that a character is going to travel from love to hate. Let us assume that there are nine emotional steps between the two poles of love and hate:

1. Love
2. Disappointment
3. Annoyance
4. Irritation
5. Disillusionment
6. Indifference
7. Disgust
8. Anger
9. Hate

If a character goes from No. 1 to No. 4, this constitutes jumping conflict. The author has neglected to show transitional steps Nos. 2 and 3. If the character then goes from No. 4 to No. 6, this is again jumping, because step No. 5 has been left out.

In real life a person may go through emotional changes in lightning-like fashion, so much so that his decision seems jumpy or hasty. This is not so. He has really gone through all the transitional steps, but so rapidly that it is not apparent. In fiction every step must be obvious and clearly shown.

When each character goes through each step, No. 1 to No. 10, then we have slowly rising conflict. Remember that each step must be higher than the succeeding one, just as each act gathers more momentum than the one before until the final curtain is reached.

CRISIS, CLIMAX, RESOLUTION

A play or story from beginning to end is a series of crises, climaxes, and resolutions. It begins with a crisis and builds up from there.

The crisis is a turning point, a time when a change is imminent. For example, in childbirth the birth pains are the crisis, the birth is the climax, and the resolution is life or death.

Do you remember the play *Rope's End,* by Patrick Hamilton? Two rich young men murder their schoolmate for the thrill and experience. As the curtain rises, they, the killers, are seen stuffing the murdered youth into a large chest. They invite the murdered youth's father in for a discussion in order to experience the thrill and danger that his visit will produce.

The play starts with a crisis, as all plays and all good fiction writing should. A crisis is an unknown quantity, a turning point.

As the conflict in a play rises to meet each new crisis, climax, and resolution, the author keeps building for the final crisis, climax, and resolution, which will be the sum total of all the other crises, climaxes, and resolutions, proving the premise.

The first crisis is a minor one and proceeds to the second and third till it arrives at the greatest and final crisis.

If each succeeding crisis does not rise on an ascending scale, the conflict becomes static.

The final crisis, climax, and resolution can follow each other in rapid order at the end of the play, or an interval can exist between them. In *A Doll's House* almost all of the third act constitutes resolution, as Nora explains to Helmer why she cannot remain. Even this resolution keeps transcending until the proud Helmer begs her forgiveness and begs Nora to stay. At this time a new crisis is created. Her refusal is the climax, and her departure the resolution.

The same principles apply to short stories and novels. While a short story consists of only one or two episodes, a novel may have hundreds, one after the other.

In a short story the tempo marches quickly, while in the novel it ambles along. But crisis, climax, and resolution are at work on the same general principle found in playwriting. Following are famous novelists and playwrights and their works for reference:

Bennett, Arnold	THE OLD WIVES' TALE
Bowen, Elizabeth	THE DEATH OF THE HEART
Cather, Willa	MY ANTONIA
	DEATH COMES FOR THE
	ARCHBISHOP
	A LOST LADY
Conrad, Joseph	NOSTROMO
	THE NIGGER OF THE NARCISSUS
	VICTORY

Dickens, Charles	DAVID COPPERFIELD
Dos Passos, John	U.S.A. *(The 42nd Parallel 1919 The Big Money)*
Dostoievsky, Fyodor	THE BROTHERS KARAMAZOV
Dreiser, Theodore	AN AMERICAN TRAGEDY SISTER CARRIE
Faulkner, William	THE WILD PALMS INTRUDER IN THE DUST
France, Anatole	PENGUIN ISLAND THAIS THE CRIME OF SYLVESTRE BONNARD
Fitzgerald, F. Scott	THE GREAT GATSBY TENDER IS THE NIGHT
Forster, E. M.	A PASSAGE TO INDIA
Galsworthy, John	THE FORSYTE SAGA
Glasgow, Ellen	VEIN OF IRON
Gide, André	THE COUNTERFEITERS
Hemingway, Ernest	A FAREWELL TO ARMS THE SUN ALSO RISES FOR WHOM THE BELL TOLLS
Huxley, Aldous	POINT COUNTER POINT
James, Henry	THE PORTRAIT OF A LADY THE AMBASSADORS WASHINGTON SQUARE
Joyce, James	ULYSSES

Kipling, Rudyard	JUNGLE BOOKS SOLDIERS THREE THE LIGHT THAT FAILED
Lewis, Sinclair	ARROWSMITH MAIN STREET BABBITT
London, Jack	THE CALL OF THE WILD
Mann, Thomas	BUDDENBROOKS THE MAGIC MOUNTAIN
Maugham, W. Somerset	OF HUMAN BONDAGE
Melville, Herman	MOBY DICK
Proust, Marcel	REMEMBRANCE OF THINGS PAST
Rolland, Romain	JEAN CHRISTOPHE
Tolstoi, Leo	WAR AND PEACE ANNA KARENINA
Twain, Mark	TOM SAWYER HUCKLEBERRY FINN
Undset, Sigrid	KRISTIN LAVRANSDATTER
Wells, H. G.	TONO-BUNGAY
Wharton, Edith	THE AGE OF INNOCENCE ETHAN FROME
Wilder, Thornton	THE BRIDGE OF SAN LUIS REY
Wolfe, Thomas	LOOK HOMEWARD, ANGEL
Woolf, Virginia	MRS. DALLOWAY
Zola, Émile	GERMINAL

PLAYS

Barrie, Sir James M.	WHAT EVERY WOMAN KNOWS
Barry, Philip	THE PHILADELPHIA STORY
Boothe, Clare	THE WOMEN
Chekhov, Anton	THE CHERRY ORCHARD
Connelly, Marc	THE GREEN PASTURES
Galsworthy, John	LOYALTIES
Green, Paul	IN ABRAHAM'S BOSOM
Gregory, Lady Augusta	THE RISING OF THE MOON
Hauptmann, Gerhart	THE WEAVERS
Hecht, Ben & MacArthur, Charles	THE FRONT PAGE
Hellman, Lillian	THE LITTLE FOXES
Housman, Laurence	VICTORIA REGINA
Howard, Sidney	THE SILVER CORD YELLOW JACK THEY KNEW WHAT THEY WANTED
Kaufman, George S.	THE ROYAL FAMILY
Kelly, George	CRAIG'S WIFE
Kesselring, Joseph	ARSENIC AND OLD LACE
Kingsley, Sidney	DEAD END
Kober, Arthur	HAVING WONDERFUL TIME
Lindsay, Howard & Crouse, Russel	LIFE WITH FATHER
Maeterlinck, Maurice	PELLEAS AND MELISANDE

Maugham, W. Somerset	THE CIRCLE
Milne, A. A.	MR. PIM PASSES BY
Odets, Clifford	AWAKE AND SING
	GOLDEN BOY
	WAITING FOR LEFTY
O'Neill, Eugene	AH! WILDERNESS
Percy, Edward & Denham, Reginald	LADIES IN RETIREMENT
Pinero, Sir Arthur Wing	THE SECOND MRS. TANQUERAY
Sheriff, R. C.	JOURNEY'S END
Sherwood, Robert E.	ABE LINCOLN IN ILLINOIS
	IDIOT'S DELIGHT
	THE PETRIFIED FOREST
Spewack, Bella & Samuel	BOY MEETS GIRL
Steinbeck, John	OF MICE AND MEN
Strindberg, August	THE FATHER
Synge, John Millington	RIDERS TO THE SEA
Vane, Sutton	OUTWARD BOUND
Wilde, Oscar	LADY WINDERMERE'S FAN
Williams, Emlyn	NIGHT MUST FALL
	THE CORN IS GREEN
Williams, Tennessee	THE GLASS MENAGERIE

And the collected works of:
    George Bernard Shaw
    Eugene O'Neill
    John Galsworthy
    Lillian Hellman

APPENDIX II

A Short Cut to Enjoying and Criticizing Plays, Films, and Television Shows

Six men have the power in New York to decide whether a play should live or die. They are decent and honorable men, these six. I believe implicitly that there is not one iota of malice in them, and still, if they happen to dislike a play, that play is doomed. On the other hand, if they love the play, every one around the theatre will make money and the dramatist will become famous.

Whose fault is it that six, good, capable men should be the sole judges, and the arbiters or the executioners in the name of 8,000,000 people, and decide what play should live or die?

This power has been given to them by the people of New York.

If anything is wrong with this system of reporting, the responsibility lies not with those who report, but with those who have relegated the power to a few to judge, to select suitable plays for them to enjoy.

How can six men know what 8,000,000 people are going to love or reject tomorrow? The temper of one man or many is mercurial, in a constant flux. No one can say with authority how the people are going to feel tomorrow.

Economic forces, the threat of war, or any national calamity, such as a depression or an inflation, can influence the temper of people so thoroughly that it can mean the complete reversal of what the majority wished or clamored for twenty-four hours earlier.

The public is lazy and negligent. They seem to say "Let someone else tell us what we should wear, do, eat, see, or hear. Our sole purpose in life is to make a living. Let others who know better tell us the rest."

Such irresponsible behavior means abdicating the power of thinking, of reasoning, of selecting, of being a man. To forage like an animal, to connive, to steal, even kill for food, is an inborn atavistic instinct of the herd to live, but it is not the sole aim of the man who fought his way up from the primeval ooze, to be master over all that lives on this earth.

To think is to be alive.

Not to think is to be dead.

This section will help the man who has the strength and who wishes to arrogate for himself his birthright, to select and enjoy a play, movie, or TV show without anyone telling him first whether it fits his taste or not.

It is a grand feeling to be grown up, to be mature, and to think for oneself at last.

The undying popularity of baseball springs from the spectators' intimate knowledge of the game. By knowing the three dimensions of a human being and the structure of a play, the audience too can follow the intricate pattern with the greatest ease, and such intimacy will enhance the appetite of the public to go more often to the theatre, not only to enjoy, but to match wits with the professional reviewers.

The influence of the reviewers would not necessarily be diminished by the audience's understanding of a play. They could remain as impressive as before, only the power of being the law and the executioner of the theatre would be taken away from them forever.

THE SHORT CUT

Curiosity is man's inherent characteristic. If you happen to pass two quarreling people on the street—if you are part of the majority—you would like to know what the quarrel is about.

It is important for you to find out as soon as the play starts what the author intends to say to you.

There are two main forces that struggle against each other on the stage, the *Protagonist* and the *Antagonist*.

If you remember this, you shall understand the intricacies, the structure of any kind of play, let it be a sordid drama, comedy, or farce. Even fairy tales conform to this rule.

The Protagonist sooner or later starts the conflict. If he starts late, then there is one strike against the play. People don't go to the theatre to hear polite conversation. They expect suspense and conflict.

How do you recognize the Protagonist?

He starts the conflict.

For whatever reason one holds a grudge, suspicion, legal or illegal claim against another, if he is willing to prosecute him to the limit, he is the Protagonist.

The aggressor is always the Protagonist.

If the Protagonist forgets his grouch, suspicion, or whatever he has against his adversary, the play starts to die.

Why does the audience always demand conflict in the theatre?

Because no human being will expose himself without conflict. No character can show his inner turmoil, contradiction, vacillation, self-doubt, hate, or love to the audience without *attacking* or *defending* himself.

Everyone of us has a thousand faces.

Which is the real one?

Without conflict we'll never find out.

Since we wish to find out the motivation, the nature of the Protagonist, he should be provoked by the Antagonist's refusal of his demands.

The *Antagonist* is the other force, besides the Protagonist, who sparks the conflict; he is willing to fight, struggle, to connive, to undermine, to divert the attention of the Protagonist.

Without the Protagonist the Antagonist has no reason to exist.

Neither the Protagonist nor the Antagonist can exist without each other.

No shadow can exist without light, and vice-versa.

Life has no meaning without struggle; struggle is the essence, the foundation, the means of existence.

Every action creates a counter action. It should be a chain reaction which goes on interminably in an ascending scale.

All conflict in all plays (as has been true in the past and will be true in the future) is *for or against the status quo.*

Any small squabble, insult, little or big war (and this includes the two World Wars) started *for* or *against* the status quo.

The Protagonist is always against the Antagonist. *This is the essence, the bone structure of all writing.*

Their struggle takes many forms—simple or complicated, symbolic or real. But whatever form they take, don't forget the conflict is between the Protagonist and the Antagonist, and must go on if the play is to live.

The play, any play, is supposed to be the mirror of life.

Struggle is the essence of life.

If you know the rules of the game, you will enjoy yourselves better than just waiting in the theatre to be stirred and entertained.

You are watching two people fight in the arena; one is the Protagonist, the other is the Antagonist.

If the Protagonist is so strong, so overwhelming that there is no doubt in your mind who is going to win, the result will be boredom.

The combatants should be evenly matched.

The Antagonist should not be submissive either, or so frightened that you are sure he will be smashed, destroyed even before the fight is started. The effect will be the same as before. You will lose interest.

The evenly matched combatants almost immediately create suspense.

The play, movie, or TV show must concern itself with the problems of man: love, hate, avarice, suspicion, ambition, or any other of the myriad fears that beset all mortals.

Man is a complex entity. He goes to the theatre not only for entertainment, but to understand himself. Since all human emotion is universal, he will compare his with that of others. Whichever problem the author chooses to write about, he must dig deep, to the very root of struggle, to be true.

Here was a man who was jealous of his wife.

It was obvious that he was jealous, but it was not so obvious why he was jealous.

Did she take him for granted? No.

Did she feel superior and treat him as a poor relation? No.

Did she flirt? No.

Was she unfaithful to him? Positively not.

On top of all this, she was kind, softspoken, and in love with her husband.

Then why, in heaven's name, was he jealous?

I quote: "I never finished elementary school and I am making money by the carload, while you with your fancy degrees can't get more from that crummy two-bit library job than seventy bucks a week."

She didn't answer his taunting, sarcastic, dirty digs. He never made her forget that he was supposed to be an ignoramus, a man who never read a book and was proud of it, yet could get a woman like her to crawl after him.

They had three children, and through the years he made

her disillusioned, bitter, even desperate. She devoutly wished for a divorce or widowhood as preferable to continuing to live with this ruthless, jealous man.

He was jealous of her intellectual integrity. He was jealous not of men, but of seeing her read a book. Any book was his adversary.

He was relentless. He constantly tried to undermine her importance and prove to her, and to himself of course, that higher learning was the bunk. A clever man didn't need school or books to succeed. He wished to prove his superiority not only above her, but above schools.

All Protagonists are, by sheer necessity, relentless—for whatever reasons—and the Antagonists, if they intend to stay alive, must fight back. The Antagonists perhaps fumble at first, but slowly, under the ruthless onslaughts of the Protagonists, will protest, reject, refuse, and at the end revolt.

Every human being fights constantly for his or her superiority.

The importance of being important is the equivalent of self-preservation.

What else should we know about the Protagonist? Why is he the Protagonist?

If you really want to enjoy the play and know how to criticize it, study the following diagram:

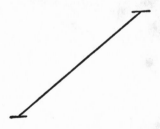

The above line tells you that every play, movie, or TV play should be built on slowly rising conflict.

Slowly rising means without interruption, moving higher and higher, like 1, 2, 3, 4, 5, 6, 7, 8, 9, 0.

The conflict starts at 1, and proceeds in ascending scale up to 0, which is the end of the play.

Now, if the conflict bogs down, at let us say 1 or 4, or any other number, the play will be static.

Staticness is the deadly disease of creative writing.

If the play is going to jump, let us say from 3 to 7, or 5 to 8, or any other span, it will create an unhealthy reaction. The play has lost the touch of reality, has left logic, the right kind of motivation, behind. This is the cause of the jumping conflict.

The slowly rising conflict is the answer for a healthy, well-constructed play.

Let me illustrate the static conflict:

Staticness by its own weight sinks lower and lower to the vanishing point, where the audience loses interest and doesn't give a hoot about what is going to happen to the people in the play.

A jumping conflict might look like this:

It is erratic.

Mood and logic change so quickly, the conflict loses all semblance of reality.

If you keep in mind that the two main forces in every dramatic composition are the oft-repeated Protagonist and Antagonist, cumbersome explanations will not be necessary to understand any play, movie, or TV drama.

Every Protagonist forces the conflict throughout the play. *He always knows what he wants.* Iago in *Othello*, revenge; Macbeth, ambition; and Tartuffe, lust. Whatever the Protagonist wants, he must want it so badly that he will destroy or be destroyed in the attempt to get it. But no real Protagonist will start a conflict because of a whim. Necessity drives him.

Once more, please, dear reader, remember that necessity drives the Protagonist on and on.

If there is no unbreakable bond between the two main forces, they are likely to walk out on each other. (This is a beautiful contradiction. The seemingly unbreakable bond should break by death, or a dramatic change in a situation of a character at the end of the play.)

The unbreakable bond is created by great love, great hate, hurt ego, revenge, or any other emotion you can think of, if you put before the emotion the word "great." It must be really great.

Only a great uncontrollable drive, a compulsive force, can carry the Protagonist through a three-act play. You never saw a good play in which the Protagonist remained complacent.

Conflict is the heartbeat of every play. Conflict is the oxygen, the food for a play to thrive on. Without conflict there is no play, and in reality there would be no life on earth either.

If conflict doesn't grow in intensity, the play will drag and become repetitious. You will find the play falling apart.

SUMMARY

1) How does one recognize a three-dimensional character? Very simply. Through conflict.

2) Let me repeat. Every man has a thousand faces. Only through conflict can layer after layer be peeled off, until you find the real man or woman crouching behind the façade.

3) The moment the play opens, find the Protagonist. It is easy to recognize him. He starts the conflict.

4) The Antagonist stands right there, at the opposite corner.

5) The perfect opening for a play is to start with a *crisis*, which grows in intensity and explodes into a *climax*.

6) Static Conflict, the deadly sickness of all plays, occurs if the characters are weighted down with repetitious dialogue.

7) Jumping Conflict is the sign of lack of motivation. Without motivation characters become straw men.

8) If there is no strong bond between the characters, there is no good reason to fight. They simply can walk out from the action, and the play ends before it starts.

9) The rest of the characters in the play will side with one or the other of the combatants.

A play is really a mirror; whoever looks into it will be reflected back, not as he looks, or as others see him, but as he sees himself at the moment.

THIS IS ALL